BREAKING SIN'S GRASP

YOUR TEMPTATION DOESN'T DEFINE YOU

JIM DOMEN

BREAKING SIN'S GRASP, *Your Temptation Doesn't Define You*

Copyright 2024 by Jim Domen.

All Rights Reserved

Published by Leadership Books, Inc., Las Vegas, NV – New York, NY
LeadershipBooks.com

ISBN:
978-1-951648-86-2 (Hardcover)
978-1-951648-87-9 (Paperback)
978-1-951648-88-6 (eBook)

All Rights Reserved. No part of this publication may be reproduced, distributed, or transmitted in any form or by any means, including photocopying, recording, or other electronic or mechanical methods, without the prior written permission of the publisher, except in the case of brief quotations embodied in critical reviews and certain other noncommercial uses permitted by copyright law.

Leadership Books, Inc., is committed to publishing works of quality and integrity. In that spirit, we are proud to offer this book to our readers; however, the story, the experiences, and the words are the author's alone. The conversations in the book all come from the author's recollections, not word-for-word transcripts. All of the events are true to the best of the author's memory. The author, in no way, represents any company, corporation, or brand mentioned herein. The views expressed are solely those of the author.

All Scripture quotations, unless otherwise indicated, are taken from the *Holy Bible, New International Version*®, NIV® Copyright ©1973, 1978, 1984, 2011 by Biblica, Inc.® Used by permission. All rights reserved worldwide.

TABLE OF CONTENTS

Foreword ix

Introduction 1

Chapter 1: Realize Why You Aren't Free 9

Chapter 2: Reach Out to a Church 29

Chapter 3: Ride with Other Men 43

Chapter 4: Reorganize Your Schedule 55

Chapter 5: Replace Bad Habits 71

Chapter 6: Retrain Your Brain 85

Chapter 7: Rise Above 101

Final Encouragements 125

Author's Note 137

About The Author 139

ENDORSEMENTS

Lust had control on my life. No matter what I tried I just couldn't break free. Every attempt ended in failure. I had reached a point where I felt my only options were to try and minimize it or just live with it. Then I read Jim's book, and he showed me the path to freedom from lust. The irony is that I clung to lust because I thought it brought me happiness. The reality is happiness came when I broke lust's grasp.

Rich
Retired Officer US Air Force, Alaska

Pastor Jim Domen has provided men the pathway to life! I found his book very enlightening and moving! It is more applicable to my life, currently, than you may know. It was a very refreshing and motivating book to read! Through his seven-step process and the humility of actual, individual struggles; Jim offers a road map to redemption from our sins. As men and humans, we all struggle with temptation and sin. The following words give us guidance to break sin's grasp, embrace God's will, and be the leaders that God intended us to be. This book should be the foundation for all men, those who wish to embrace the Holy Spirit and choose freedom.

John
Fireman, Captain, Orange County Fire Authority, California

To say I've been caught in the unbreakable cycle is an understatement. I had hoped being married would put my desires within the bounds of being acceptable but that hasn't been the case. Coming back to Christ three years ago and getting baptized helped, but after some time I fell back into the same struggle.

I think the worst part is not feeling saved. Not feeling renewed. Not feeling the Holy Spirit. I want more than anything to feel alive in Christ and dead to myself. But I do what I hate and not what I want to do. I have so many triggers I don't even know where to start.
David
General Sales Manager, Washington

I still really struggle with imposter syndrome in the workspace so when it creeps into my personal life, I must check myself. I think a lot of men suffer from imposter syndrome and having a group of like-minded men and seeing the struggle of other brothers helps soothe or correct that.
Erich
Cyber Security Expert, San Diego, California

Breaking Sin's Grasp is a much-needed roadmap for our current generation. Jim dives into the steps to freedom from sin and the importance of relationships in our walk with Christ. This book fills the need and gives poignant insight to real growth.
Kyle
EMT (Emergency Medical Technician) Ventura, California

I am retired from public service and have been a friend of Jim for more than 20 years. During those years we have shared in Bible study, small groups, family gatherings and shared in prayer and accountability groups. What a great subject Jim took on with his most recent book, *Breaking*

ENDORSEMENTS

Sin's Grasp, Your Temptation Doesn't Define You. We are currently living in a world full of challenges and darkness. If you are a person of faith, then you know Jesus was and always will be the only one without sin. No one is perfect and no one is free of mistakes. This book addresses a number of areas in life which leads us to dark or isolated places in life, and offers ways for us to overcome the darkness, mend relationships, and help us grow in relationships, especially in relationship with God. Wherever you currently see yourself, faith-based or not, this read has something for you. A book filled with hope and help, this book would be perfect for a Bible study, a group environment surrounding, a retreat and/or counseling environment. As a son, brother, husband, father and friend I was encouraged through this book, and found ways I can provide support and encouragement for others struggling or looking for more in their lives. This book will encourage you to find the light in darkness, with thoughtful and manageable ways to get there.
David, Law Enforcement Captain, Los Angeles, California

FOREWORD

I was raised as a religious non-believer. I attended church every Sunday for as long as I can remember. I don't remember a time when I didn't believe in God, but I had no personal relationship with Him. Going to church seemed to be the cultural thing to do in rural America of that era. On a positive note, my religious tradition taught me the basics of right and wrong, and I truly tried to live according to that moral code. I looked like the all-American boy with no criminal record or observable addictions. Even during my four-year tour of duty in the Navy I attended Protestant services on Sunday. However, I was exposed to an environment less than conducive to righteous living, to put it mildly.

Pornography was readily available, and masturbation became a habit I could easily hide. After being discharged from the Navy I attended college, earned a degree in electrical engineering, and then entered the workforce as an aerospace engineer. I married Joanne, a religious Catholic non-believer, while attending college. So, we compromised and joined the Episcopal church. As the senior warden of a small Episcopal Church plant, I received an invitation to attend a Lay Institute for Evangelism. I didn't even know what that was, but while learning to share my faith in that setting I quickly realized I didn't have anything to share! I gave my heart Christ that week--as did Joanne--and we wondered to ourselves, "How could we have played church all those years and totally missed the gospel?" It felt like a whole new world opened up to us.

The biggest issue I had to deal with was lust, and I can still remember the day I decided to clean up my mind. As you probably already know, the battle only intensified. At the time I read that men have some thought of sex every seven minutes on average. It seemed like I was beating that average by two to one. I wondered, "Why is it so hard to clean up our minds?" There is no struggle if one just gives in to tempting thoughts, but you know you are in a battle the moment you decide not to think those thoughts.

A lot of men have probably hoped that getting married would resolve that problem, but it doesn't. Blaming our wives for not meeting our sexual "needs" is a subtle form of abuse. The problem is within us, and the resolution can only come through the liberating power of a complete gospel. Jesus didn't just die for our sins, He came to give us eternal life, and that is not something we get when we die. You have eternal life the moment you received Him as your Lord and Savior. "He who has the Son has the life," (1 John 5:12). But forgiveness and new life in Christ are only two-thirds of the Gospel. "The Son of God appeared for this purpose, to destroy the works of the devil," (1 John 3:8). "Submit therefore to God. Resist the devil and he will flee from you," (James 4:7).

It has been my privilege to help thousands find their identity and freedom in Christ through genuine repentance and faith in God, and I can say from experience that sexual bondages are the most common and most resistant to treatment. That is why Jim Domen's work is so valuable to the Christian community. His struggle to overcome the bondage of homosexuality is heroic. He is a living example that one can live a righteous life if he truly wants to. "As many as received Him, to them He gave the right to become children of God," (John 1:12). No born-again believer is identified by their flesh patterns (2 Corinthians 5:16), and as Jim correctly states, neither does your temptation define you.

I encourage you to read *Breaking Sin's Grasp* and apply it to your life. You also can live a righteous life and discover "the peace of God, which surpasses all comprehension, will guard your hearts and your minds in Christ Jesus," (Philippians 4:7).

Neil T. Anderson
Founder and President Emeritus of Freedom in Christ Ministries

INTRODUCTION

Since, then, you have been raised with Christ, set your hearts on things above, where Christ is, seated at the right hand of God. Set your minds on things above, not on earthly things. For you died, and your life is now hidden with Christ in God. When Christ, who is your life, appears, then you also will appear with him in glory.

Put to death, therefore, whatever belongs to your earthly nature: sexual immorality, impurity, lust, evil desires and greed, which is idolatry. Because of these, the wrath of God is coming. You used to walk in these ways, in the life you once lived. But now you must also rid yourselves of all such things as these: anger, rage, malice, slander, and filthy language from your lips. Do not lie to each other, since you have taken off your old self with its practices and have put on the new self, which is being renewed in knowledge in the image of its Creator. There is no Gentile or Jew, circumcised or uncircumcised, barbarian, Scythian, slave or free, but Christ is all, and is in all.

Colossians 3:1-11

Men always want to ask this question: "Are you still tempted?" Everyone has a battle!

After spending five years in the gay lifestyle, luxuriating, yet living in an abusive relationship with the man who was my lover, I walked away in the summer of 2002 and returned to Jesus. In my twenty-plus years of serving Christ since then, I have not physically acted out on my old same-sex attractions. Although I sometimes struggle against same-sex desires, I can honestly say that through the divine power of God's Spirit, the truth of God's Word and the loving help of godly voices speaking sanity into my life, I have walked in freedom and continue to break the grasp of sin which previously held me captive.

Many in the secular world might label my story a "mistake." They cannot understand how a guy like me could genuinely be gay, but then become so "new in Christ" that I can now enjoy a rich and wonderful marriage with my wife, Amanda. It truly is astounding that the Father delivered me from "the domain of darkness and transferred me into the Kingdom of His Beloved Son," (Colossians 1:13). But that is the marvel of my testimony. God is greater than the urges that lurk inside of me.

My personal mission statement is "To urge men to choose life." Because I have been transformed by Christ, I have helped numerous men – including coaches and mental health professionals – journey to freedom. You must understand that the power that broke sin's grasp physically in my life is not my power. It is the power of God. So, when I urge men to choose life, I wake men up to God. Every man has it in him to choose. I respect that deeply. Men feel a longing that drives us to try to get it filled. It is deep within all men. That longing is our brokenness, our fallen nature that separates us from God. The only way to fill the hole, the urges that you have within you, is to choose life by choosing God. Your unmet needs can only be met by God. Your brokenness can only be healed by your Heavenly Father who is longing to transfer you into the kingdom of His beloved Son, and to make you His son, too. In the normal business of life, we miss out on fully addressing the drives that try to take us down and trick us into believing that we, as men, can fight and win without turning completely to God.

God is greater than the urges that lurk inside of me.

God doesn't jump in and do everything for you. God knows that you're a man (or a woman if you're a female reading this book). God respects that

INTRODUCTION

you, yourself, are going to have to decide whether you want to choose life or not. When you say "yes" and you mean it, you then relate to God *as God* and humbly let God treat you as a man (since you are not God). Both the breaking of old habits and establishing new ones take time. In fact, doing so requires a minimum of 90 days coupled with an ongoing commitment and decision to put off your "old self" and "put on your new self" by embracing your new identity in Christ. This is not a journey for the faint of heart! It is, however, a journey that many — including me — have traveled and found incredibly rewarding.

In my own power, most assuredly, I would still be pursuing whatever felt "natural" to me. I would know *nothing* of the peace and joy that come from walking in step with Jesus. But because of Christ's work in me, I am able to give God credit where credit is due. I'm not claiming to be someone who is "good at being a Christian." I'm saying that my God is good at being my God.

My story never grows old. Each time I share, I continue to witness the ways that God transforms a life. He broke the grasp of sin on my life, and He has done it with countless others, and I have every confidence He can do it with you.

I'm not claiming to be someone who is "good at being a Christian." I'm saying that my God is good at being my God.

I've been in ministry for over 20 years, having walked with both men and women dealing with various sin issues. In my ministry career, I've served on pastoral staff in men's ministry, so naturally I worked with men and, as a result, all but one example used in this book are men's stories. Ladies, this does not discount you or the sin issues with which you wrestle. The pathway to freedom is the same for everyone even though your preferences and temptations could be different than the stories illustrated in *Breaking Sin's Grasp*.

If you find yourself caught in a cycle of habitual sin, I have good news to share. Freedom awaits you! Whether you're a guy in your late teens, young adult years, or more "mature" like me, the principles of freedom remain the same.

In the early 90s, I recall hearing the great Catholic theologian, Henri Nouwen, speak at George Fox College, where I pursued undergraduate studies. The title of his book, *The Wounded Healer*, always resonated with me. Everyone has wounds because everyone is broken. But the wonder of God is that He can take even the most broken individuals and use them to bless others. As Nouwen writes, "What is most personal and unique in each one of us is probably the very element which would, if it were shared or expressed, speak most deeply to others."[1] I pray that my journey, along with the lessons I have learned, impacts your life in a similar way.

The steps to freedom I offer come from a heart that knows what it means to be wounded by sin and offered restoration by the Grand Healer. I am far from perfect. I have not arrived. Like everyone, I'm in need of a Savior, and the longer I've served as a speaker and coach to men, the more I have realized everyone faces their own battles. For some, their struggle glares on full display. Others wage a battle in their minds as they wrestle with secret sins in private. Regarding the thousands of men and women to whom I've spoken, very few are proud of their sinful lifestyles. They want to break free, but they just don't know how.

I can empathize because I didn't know how either. That's part of my story too. When I first recommitted my life to Christ, I worried about what others would think. I figured that I would be judged and ranked as a second-class Christian. While some of my dread certainly did materialize

---

[1] Henri J.M. Nouwen, The Wounded Healer: Ministry in Contemporary Society

INTRODUCTION

into some painful moments, to my surprise in coming out and my committed intention to break "out" of sin's grasp, I received an overwhelming response of love and acceptance from my family in Christ (what the New Testament often calls "the body of Christ"). After breaking my silence and sharing with others all the shame of my struggles, I experienced an incredibly life-giving sense of freedom and soon began to share my story publicly, from a stage. I just went up in front of everyone and told the truth and did not make any excuses for myself. I was vulnerable, not pretentious. Super honest. And when I did that, I watched man after man come to the front, after the service, to offer their own confessions.

Older men would tell me about an affair they had just committed against their wives. Middle-aged men would share how they had grown unfulfilled in their marriage and started looking at pornography. Younger men, in their early twenties, would share about the difficulty of saving their virginity for marriage. Every one of them, young and old, could tell a story.

Like the sinful woman in Luke 7, we, as men, can love Christ much because He has forgiven us much. Jesus makes the point plain and simple. In the New Testament Gospel of Luke, Jesus said to a religious leader, Simon, "A certain moneylender had two debtors, one owed five hundred denarii, and the other fifty. When they were unable to repay, he graciously forgave them both. Which of them, therefore, will love him more?" You and I are empowered to love God more because He has forgiven us of so much! You and I can increase in our love for others when we think of all that Christ has done for us. I like to say it out loud: *I am able to love much because I have been forgiven much.*

In this book, I will share not only a list of principles for breaking sin's grasp on your life, but I will introduce you to the stories of other men transformed by the power of God. You will hear dramatic stories of transformation, such as that of a former stripper, and a drug dealer-addict who became a godly pastor. You will also read stories of continued heartbreak and failure. I intend to be real, authentic, and genuine with my own journey and the journeys of hundreds of men I've counseled, journeyed alongside, and coached. I hope God uses these stories to encourage, sharpen, and build *you* into a mighty warrior: a warrior for the Kingdom of God, a warrior as a husband, a warrior as a father, and a warrior as a son.

You do not have to live as a slave to sin. You can experience the wonderful liberation that happens when you live as a child — a son — of God. As Deuteronomy 30:19-20 instructs, "Choose life, so that you and your children may live and that you may love the Lord your God, listen to his voice, and hold fast to him."

You do not have to live as a slave to sin.

Ultimately, experiencing the freedom and life God offers comes down to a choice. One passage in the Bible I often reference is John 5, when Jesus is in Jerusalem at the pool of Bethesda. Many sick people would gather there in hopes they would one day be healed. At the Pool of Bethesda, the following account unfolds in the first nine verses:

After this there was a feast of the Jews, and Jesus went up to Jerusalem.

Now there is in Jerusalem by the Sheep Gate a pool, in Aramaic called Bethesda, which has five roofed colonnades. In these lay a multitude of invalids — blind, lame, and paralyzed. One man was there who had been an invalid for thirty-eight years. When Jesus saw him lying there and knew that he had already been there a long time, he said to him, "Do you want to be healed?" The sick man answered him, "Sir, I have no one to put me into the pool when the water is stirred. While I am trying to get in, someone else goes down ahead of me." Jesus said to him, "Get up!

INTRODUCTION

Pick up your mat and walk." And at once the man was healed, and he took up his bed and walked.[2]

"Do you want to be healed?" These are the critical words this man had to answer and the same question we face today. When our desires get out of alignment with obedience to Christ, and our wants stray from his desires, we end up in trouble. As a result of our determination to go our own way, God often doesn't fight us but permits us to make our own choices outside of His intended will. Each of us struggles with different hurts and hang-ups, but when we encounter Jesus, we are all confronted with the same question: "Do you *want* to be healed?" Do you *want* to be free?

If you do, it is time to understand what is holding you back.

---

[2] English Standard Version

CHAPTER 1

REALIZE WHY YOU AREN'T FREE

> You, my brothers and sisters, were called to be free. But do not use your freedom to indulge the flesh; rather, serve one another humbly in love. For the entire law is fulfilled in keeping this one command: "Love your neighbor as yourself." If you bite and devour each other, watch out or you will be destroyed by each other. So I say, walk by the Spirit, and you will not gratify the desires of the flesh. For the flesh desires what is contrary to the Spirit, and the Spirit what is contrary to the flesh. They are in conflict with each other, so that you are not to do whatever you want.
>
> *Galatians 5:13-17*

It all started when I viewed a pornographic image for the first time. On a warm summer day, still in the fourth grade, and on the eve of my puberty years, I set off one afternoon with a few of my buddies on one of our many childhood excursions. Our first stop was Tuffree Park, a fun oasis innocently tucked in a quiet neighborhood that was waiting for us kids to fulfill our thirst for adventure.

Back in the 1980s, it was normal for kids to live with a sense of blissful freedom and naivete. Like Andy Griffith's wholesome town of Mayberry, our California city of Placentia was a place where everyone watched out for each other. There wasn't all the talk we see and hear on the news today of child abductions. Parents thought little of allowing their kids to roam the streets in search of another adventure. Kids were allowed to be kids. My little band of brothers on our BMX bikes cycled past the snack shack, then past the Little League ballpark and ventured further into the community known as Tri City Park. There we took full advantage of our liberty to play and explore without being hampered or censored. The only rule we had to follow was this: Be home before the streetlights came on.

Next, we arrived at a small enclave of trees where we skidded to a halt because we stumbled across what looked to be someone's treasure trove – a magazine collection. But these were not clothing catalogs; they were pornographic magazines full of fleshy photos that made our hearts pound. Apparently, someone in our community, lacking a hiding place in their decent American home, needed to stash this explicit material somewhere else nearby, so they used this spot as an "under the mattress" location to store their treasure trove of indecent material not meant for every eye to see.

Since we were prepubescent and thinking of sex as more than a little gross, all the rest of the boys in my group took one look at the stack and sojourned on their merry way, shaking their heads in bewilderment at the bizarre things adults apparently considered to be pleasurable. But I lingered behind. Something about these images struck a chord in me. I had seen porn once before but nothing like this.

Before the digital era, one would rarely stumble upon images like these. Back then, you couldn't just click your way around on the Internet or see pop-ups on your mobile device. The images I saw were way too taboo for anyone to find easily. To find material like this in the 1980s you had to look for it secretly and watch your back as you searched.

The Start of a Fascination

One glance at these magazine images aroused in me an insatiable desire that overtook my spirit because I was so enamored by the naked bodies. As my buddies continued to ride over the rolling hills that were matted with dry tree roots, I stayed behind under the shady enclave, where time itself seemed to stand still. What felt like an hour was probably only five minutes as my fascination grew with every turn of the page. I could hear happy voices fading in the background as my friends kept riding further distances away. But I devoted my focus entirely to the images before me.

Nude pictures aroused more than my curiosity; it ignited in me an excitement I had never felt. At once, a mixture of excitement and embarrassment washed over my sense of identity and left me feeling thrilled yet unsettled. Even at the tender age of ten, I knew how the basics of life were supposed to work. Boys were not supposed to view such material. "Jimmy, are you joining us?" I heard one of the boys shout. Laying the magazines aside, I picked up my bike from which I had dismounted, then scrambled to catch up with the boys. I was part of the group. Being boys, we spent the rest of that afternoon zipping through the woods, hooting and hollering as kids do. No one thought to ask me anything else. Why would they? Who cares why I was delayed? The episode was mine. It happened in isolation. I was oblivious as well. On that day, I never could have imagined how my secret experience would leave a lasting imprint on my life.

Little did I know that my fourth-grade indulgence was an unmarked gateway into a whole new world: a world of sexual fantasy that insatiably compelled me to act on strange desires that none of my friends shared. Some readers may be surprised to know that I lived the remainder of my childhood and all my teenage years as the "golden child" of my Christian family. It took time for the seeds of my private encounter with pornography to sprout a desire in me that was totally overwhelming and unhealthy.

However, my chance encounter with the paraphernalia of someone else's sin issue did not launch me into a life of being a serial porn addict. That is not my story. I never became the kid who sneaked the latest issues of *Playboy* into my parents' home. I was a good boy. I did my very best to obey every rule that my parents set in place.

Only in retrospect can I see how pivotal that one afternoon became as it played out vividly in my mind and in my life. On the surface, that encounter was occasioned in innocence–just a few young boys on a routine bike ride to the local park. I did not pursue the occasion. As a kid, you don't realize the inevitable consequences and impact of unholy encounters. I knew nothing other than that I had stumbled across something that made me feel different from any way that I had felt before.

Everyone Has a Story

While everyone's story is different, I have come to see many young men's stories parallel mine. They also recall a moment in their adolescent or young-adult years when they were exposed to something that captivated their sexual imagination and awakened a life-long battle with lust. Men will wrestle with untamed sexual appetites unless they proactively choose to put safeguards in place. The allure of pornography, sex outside of marriage (pre-marital sex or extramarital sex), the euphoria of drugs, the thrill of gambling, digital gaming, the anticipation of the next alcoholic drink, or the sheer enjoyment of some other sensual pleasure sets men on a path they never imagined they would travel.

To those who have been taken onto this path of bondage, freedom feels like a tricky and elusive reality. Whether the struggle is with power, greed, money, gambling, alcohol, drugs, pornography, sex, or some kind of infatuation with the lurid idea of having numerous sexual partners (or whatever your sin issue may be), the feeling that comes with that struggle is a feeling of hopelessness that engulfs and convinces us that we are doomed to defeat. As despair sets in, we start to believe that regardless of how hard we try, we will never be free.

Everyone has his own story. For my friend Colton (25 years old), who started looking at porn at age 18, it took seven years for him to recover. Another friend of mine is Police Officer Adam (41 years old). After a neighbor molested him, Adam spent twenty-five years struggling with porn to cope with his shame and unrelenting pain that he could not fathom telling anyone about. Everyone has a story, yet only through *understanding* our stories can we experience the freedom our souls crave. Both men had their God moments when I led them through *Steps to Freedom in Christ*. It was the Holy Spirit who revealed their root issues and broke sin's grasp.

The Holy Spirit revealed during their sessions that Adam never forgave his abuser and Colton's dad didn't prepare him. Both were lightning bolt moments. Adam was set free! And in Colton's encounter, he struggled with the regret that his dad never prepared him with actions to take if he saw pornographic images on his phone. At 25, he confessed this disappointment, "If my dad would have coached me what to do, I wouldn't have had this addiction."

Only as we remember and realize where we came from can we begin to comprehend who we can become. After counseling men with various sexual issues, I've come to know several important things. First, father and son relationships are critical. A strained, disconnected relationship with a dad can lead to a series of poor choices. Second, different men express their brokenness in different ways. For example, I've been in countless men's accountability groups where I've heard a dizzying number of struggles expressed. Yet, in each of these cases, the outward act of sin covered up a deeper root problem that was unique to each man's story. The sin was but a symptom.

BREAKING SIN'S GRASP

Only as we remember and realize where we came from can we begin to comprehend who we can become.

For example, I once counseled a man named Hunter. Through months of pastoral counseling with me, I took Hunter through many of the same steps you'll encounter in this book. No matter how much time Hunter and I spent together, I sensed he wasn't making much progress. Hunter's mom had raised him alone and he did not have the benefit of having a father at home, much less a strong relationship with his father. But during our season of one-to-one coaching and counseling, I helped Hunter learn how to do things that he had not been taught, presumably because his dad was absent. I helped him create a budget for the first time, taught him how to live within his financial means, and encouraged him so that he could see that he was capable of being financially responsible. Yet even as Hunter grew in practical areas of living his life, he nonetheless failed morally and continued to have numerous female sexual partners.

Hunter was a good-looking guy. He got hired to wait tables at a Disneyland restaurant, and Hunter had no problem picking up women there. Nearly every day, Hunter returned home from work with a new phone number, and a new sexy woman who craved his sexual attention. Unbeknownst to me at the time, Hunter also volunteered to serve in a youth group at a local church where he secretly engaged in yet more destructive behavior. As an outgoing, charismatic, handsome 24-year-old, he was idolized by many teenage girls. After a few short months of volunteering, a peer of Hunter's shared with me that Hunter had carried his same unhealthy patterns with young women to underaged girls in their mid-teens. When rumors came to light, his church ousted him appropriately and abruptly from volunteering with the youth group.

When I learned of his dismissal a few days after it happened, I could only shake my head in disgust and anger. Throughout his entire time with me, Hunter talked a good game. While saying he wanted to be free, his actions told a very different story. In theory, Hunter knew exactly how to live a righteous life. He could talk the talk. But in practice, he chose death. He chose to be a slave to his voracious lusts. He chose to lie to himself about his internal struggle. As a result, he went through the seven steps outlined in this book, but he only did so outwardly. Hunter was an actor who theatrically nodded his head in agreement with all I had said. But his life told the truth, evidenced by an unchanged man who lacked the power to resist his sexual desire.

Why People Aren't Free

I share Hunter's story as an opening word of warning. If you've been around the church for any length of time, it's easy to figure out how to work the system. You can quickly learn how to use the right jargon. You can come up with answers whenever someone starts to question your actions in an effort to give you the gift of accountability. Whenever someone starts to question your actions, you know how to distance yourself from others and deflect attention so that you can keep indulging in your sin of choice. You can dip one toe into the water of faith and still immerse your other nine toes in your favorite sin. Any run-of-the-mill sinner can plan for a quick escape if the pressure gets too intense. You say you want to follow Jesus, but inside you are unwilling to follow Him.

If this is your story, I want you to pause right now and answer this question: Do you want to be healed?

Are you at the point where you are fed up with living the way you have always lived? Or do you only want the benefits that come with Christian living? Are you trying to live the life of a disciple, yet doing so in a way divorced from the disciplines of a godly life? If this is where you are, allow me to be frank with you. There is one primary reason why most men never break free from the habit of sexual sin, and it is this: *Sin is fun!*

Hebrews 11:25 validates the truth that the pleasures of sin are enjoyable. But it also offers this thought. A three-word catch: "for a season." Sin is enjoyable, but only *for a season.* The author of Hebrews doesn't say how long this season lasts. For some, it's only a short time. For others, it might be years, even decades, of tremendous enjoyment. But that sin comes at a cost. The more sin you have, the greater the cost.

For the person who has established personal happiness as their ultimate goal, the pathway of sin might seem like a solid option. But it's important to understand that a life like this inevitably results in spiritual death and disconnection from the *One* who is the Source of everlasting joy.

I make this point because there are well-meaning Christian influencers who speak as though living in sin is always a terrible experience. From the way they speak, you might think every person who looks at porn descends into a life of poverty, drug addiction, and homelessness. For most people, however, sexual sin is fun, and the thrill they receive from it makes the pursuit of God seem like a path of drudgery.

Personally, when I lived a life of sin, I felt as though *I was living in freedom.* In my mind, I was "free" to go to bars and pick up sexual one-night stands anytime I chose. I thoroughly enjoyed my sexual partnerships and especially found the thrill of immoral relationships exhilarating. I traveled the world and enjoyed erotic experiences of bathhouses in Germany, nude beaches in Hawaii, and nude resorts. I developed a successful business and lived a fast-paced life in a thriving community that was filled with fellow sinners who were likewise indulging themselves. Having the "freedom" and ability to pursue any sexual fantasy I had, and at any time that I chose, felt like the ultimate lifestyle, the ultimate freedom, the ultimate way to exist. Like the author of Ecclesiastes, I pursued pleasure through any means possible.

And while everything looked great on the outside, on the inside I was hurting. I now equate my feelings to reality TV shows: On-screen, everyone seems happy, but the cameras fail to show underlying emotions that we have as humans, even as men. The spotlight does not shine on the truth of the human condition. Nor does the TV program convey the heaviness of the sheer weight of misery that people suffer silently in pain, despair, and loneliness. Now you're hearing my story. This was my story! Only after years of decadent, sinful living had I come to realize what my badly skewed view of freedom was. I thought I was "free" in pursuing sin, but I had yet to discover the lasting joy of true freedom.

Why Real Freedom is So Intoxicating

As someone who has lived on both sides of the aisle, I can tell you that the difference between *perceived* freedom and *actual* freedom is night and day.

Fast-forward several decades: I look back on my wasted years of sin with great regret. Today, I have an incredible wife and three wonderful children. God has blessed me with a wonderful marriage. Amanda and I make a great team; she's my helpmate! Yet, if you think about it, I am way more restricted than ever before. I have family responsibilities that leave me with less time to focus on myself, sexual restrictions that limit me to one person, but these added roles and responsibilities have graced me with fulfillment. I feel better *not* indulging myself. Who would have thunk it?

My wife Amanda is such a good helpmate. She knows how to love, and I get to be in love with her. Amanda is so special. I could go on for days telling everyone about her. But had I stayed in the grasp of sin, I would've been too blind to see her beauty. I wouldn't have had a thought of even taking her on a date.

Becoming a dad three times has been one of the most amazing journeys of my life. I love being the hero and "fun daddy" to my three children. Each night I tuck them into bed, I sing their favorite songs, including a song I made up to the tune of Frère Jacques. I start with my oldest and sing, "Daddy loves you, Daddy loves you. Yes, he does! Yes, he does! Daddy loves you, Daddy loves you. All the time, all the time." I sing this to each one of my kids and then ask them who wants to pray first. They love this routine, which has even escalated to an added rock, paper, scissors competition to determine which of the two of us prays last.

Some of the sweetest times of my day are these moments at night with my children. It's a time to thank God, praise Him, and ask for strength. It's a sacred moment to reflect on the day, be still, and listen to convicting comments from my kids, such as:

- "Daddy, you didn't talk very nicely to me."
- "You hurt my feelings."
- "Daddy, why can't you be more patient like Mommy?"

Hearing negative critiques from my kids might sound like punishment, but it's a connection. It's fulfilling because I know that my kids love me and want to bond with me by telling me how they feel.

Fulfillment comes from being a real dad. Though sometimes my kids tell me that I hurt them, more often they say things that fill me to the brim, overflowing. As a responsible father, I get to enjoy soul-fulfilling, wonderful, meaningful comments such as:

- "Daddy, you reading to me was the highlight of my day!"
- "Daddy, can we float on the river again?"
- "Can you take us to the park again?"
- "Daddy, will you play rough with us?"
- "Daddy, will you take me on a daddy-daughter date? Just you and me!"
- "Daddy, will you take me on a daddy-son adventure?"

Even more fulfilling are their deep, theological questions like, "Who created God?" or "If Jesus was a baby, who looked out for all the people?"

These comments go straight to my heart! What's truly beautiful about them is that my children can share the areas where Daddy needs improvement, but also the areas in which I bring them joy. My kids rejoice because of me. They feel joy with me as I do with them.

I share this because the lasting sense of enjoyment I receive from these moments stands in stark contrast to my days in sin when the sting of emptiness and despair followed moments of "pleasure." After a night of sexual pleasure, the "high" of my evening was always met with a hangover of guilt and shame. Underneath my seared conscience, I knew that I was not living as the person I should be. But the joys I experience today in moments with my wife and kids *are* lasting and life to my spirit, and the communion I have with God is eternal. Nothing can compare to being in the right relationship, at peace, with God.

That is not to say this new *actual* freedom has not come with a cost. It certainly has. Freedom is never free. Just as the United States has invested decades of toil and bloodshed to preserve the costly freedoms we enjoy today, freedom with God also comes at a cost. Thankfully, Jesus already paid the highest price. Because of the sacrifice He made and the blood He shed on the cross, He offers you and me the greatest freedom possible.

God has done His part to bring us freedom, not so we can freely self-indulge, but so that we can freely receive His love and share His love with each other.

Different Triggers to Slavery

The opposite of freedom is slavery, and when we live a life of sexual sin outside of God's intended design, we operate as slaves to sin.

Now, it's quite possible you would not place yourself in the same category as my friend Hunter. You might not be sleeping around with anyone you choose, and you might be doing your best to do what is right. Rather than diving into a life of sin, such as I did, your story might look more like a slow slide into sin. Yours is not the picture of one who makes a dramatic leap off a cliff. Rather, it's a series of subtle compromises that position you far from where you dreamed that you would be. You want to be free, but you feel the tug of sin and struggle to break the chains of bondage. As a result, you do not yet live in victory.

Many in this category end up making a series of right choices until something triggers them to go off the rails. Everyone is triggered in different ways, and certain triggers activate sinful behaviors. Most men deal with one of these triggers and tend to act out in their sin of choice. For example, if you become hungry, angry, lonely, tired, stressed, or depressed (I use the acronym HALTS-D), your lack of an adrenaline and dopamine rush clouds your judgment. You end up making decisions that are not life-giving.

Hungry. To this point, when I'm physically hungry I get cranky, annoyed, and irritable because I have low blood sugar. When this sense of irritation sets in and I start to get frustrated with those around me, it's not uncommon for my wife, Amanda, to stop me and say, "Jim, have you eaten?" It's funny how often this simple step can make me feel like a new person! Hunger creates anxiety, and as a Type A personality, I can easily get so focused on tasks that I forget the basic nutritional aspects of life. I need to eat! Eating good food literally helps me to be a better man.

Angry. Anger is another trigger. When someone is angry it's easy to act out on the sin-of-choice to release the tension and self-medicate. If you feel wronged and make the decision in your mind to retaliate, acting out sinfully helps rid the anger build-up, providing momentary relief for how you've been let down and disappointed. It's easy to retaliate against your spouse, children, boss, parents, and friends. But when you act on your anger and think you are only hurting others, the truth remains that you are actually hurting yourself. You are hurting them as well as yourself.

REALIZE WHY YOU AREN'T FREE

> *But when you act on your anger and think you are only hurting others, the truth remains that you are actually hurting yourself. You are hurting them as well as yourself.*

Lonely. The trigger of loneliness can make us do anything to fill the void of human relationships. Now that I have a wife and three kids, I don't feel lonely, but when I was single, it was a prominent issue. My loneliness would drive me to fill the void with a sexual encounter with another person, even though one-night stands or connecting with friends at bars ended up making me feel worse in the long-run. Quick fixes helped reduce the internal pain I felt, but only for as long as the quick fix lasted. The only way to escape the awful ache of inner loneliness is to be honest with other people and share with them out loud who you really are and take time to really learn who they are. Loneliness occurs when we are disconnected relationally from others, ourselves, and God.

Tired. Failing to get adequate sleep is another major trigger, and sleep apnea is off the charts these days. The reason proper sleep is so important is that when you are tired, your defenses are down, you can't perform on your A-game, and you end up depleting your reserves, which leads to unhealthy choices. If you do not get adequate sleep, you may passively succumb to temptation, not because you are a terrible Christian, but simply because you are tired and need some Z's. When you get overly tired, it is simply easier to give up and give in instead of fighting back by taking responsibility to manage yourself.

Stressed. I'M NOT STRESSED OUT!! Really? Signs of stress are anxiousness, tension, or pent-up anger with the inability to respond in a calm, rational way when areas of your life are (or feel like they are) out of control. Contributors to stress are likely your job, finances, marital issues, a problem child, schooling, test results, or life not going the way in which you planned. One quick stress check: do you have a death grip on the steering wheel while driving or are you clinching your toes in traffic? Stress is a significant trigger as it leads to the potential necessity to "release" the build-up in an unhealthy way.

Depressed. The feeling of depression and living with a sense of hopelessness may cause us to act in an unbalanced way. Leaning into our mood of depression and neglecting to get the help we need in this area can result in irrational decision-making. I have always been told *never* to make big life changes if you are in a depressed state. Big changes can involve decisions regarding dating, marriage, job changes, education plans, coping with tragedy, loss, and facing other kinds of life-altering decisions. [Please note, if you are dealing with clinical depression, this is a mental health concern that calls for proper psychological treatment. Sometimes medical aid is necessary, so get help if you need it.]

Everyone's triggers are different. But if you don't circumvent your unhealthy patterns, you are going to stay stuck. I have found that these six primary triggers almost always lead to sin. But still, that is no excuse. We must learn to be loving even if we're hungry, angry, lonely, tired, or depressed. But let's not make this harder than it must be. Let's take responsibility to eat, get under our anger to find out what the problem is, go to bed on time, be transparent with our family and friends, deal with stress in a life-giving way, and get help if we are depressed.

Freedom Is a Choice

Ultimately, the cure for sin starts with you and believing that you have a choice. It means understanding the reason you are *not free* is because you yourself have *chosen a life of bondage*. Making this admission is a difficult action for many. In a culture that tells us to shift the blame to someone else, it becomes even more difficult to look in the mirror and take responsibility for our actions. We are born into a fallen world. Each of us desires to go our own way and live the way we choose. We all experience areas of brokenness, where the repercussions of sin mar our lives. But from there, we have a choice: either put our faith in Christ, repent from our own way, accept God's gift of salvation, and trust Him for the strength we need to walk out our commitment to Christ; or we can give in to the fleshly, sinful and selfish desires we face. Galatians 5:16 calls this "gratifying the desires of the flesh."

> *Ultimately, the cure for sin starts with you and believing that you have a choice.*

Unfortunately, many of the books I have read on the topic of sin tend to emphasize sin *management* versus sin *eradication*. As a result, we can become good at sin *compartmentalization* and experts at managing our selfishness. We may act one way with our church friends on Sunday and live a very different way at our workplace on Tuesday. At home, we may bear the image of the loving family man. But on the road, we may be looking at porn or seeking out a sexual affair.

> *Sin → Confess → Repent → Fail → Fall into Bondage → Repeat the Cycle*

We do not walk in freedom because each time we give into temptation, we promise ourselves, God, and those closest to us that "I will do better." We tell ourselves, "This time things will be different." Still, almost nothing changes. Writer Neil Anderson believes the reason for this is that we have bought into an *incomplete gospel*.

> "Many Christians are struggling because they understand only one-third of the gospel. They believe that Jesus is the Messiah who died for their sins, and if they receive Christ, their sins

will be forgiven, and they will go to heaven when they die. Such a statement is not wrong, but it is incomplete, and it gives the impression that eternal life is something believers get when they die. But the truth is that you get eternal life, starting right now! Think about it: if you wanted to save a dead man and had the power to do it, what would you do? Give him life? If that is all you did, he would only die again. To save the dead man, you would have to do two things: Save him from death and save him from being able to die again."[3]

Christ has done this for you. Yes, freedom at first feels arduous and painful, but remember that it brings joy soon after that. It has the opposite effect of sin that feels pleasurable at first, but then bites you with pain sometime afterward. Choosing life is hard when all you really care about is yourself and how you feel. But when you absorb God's love and start caring about God and caring about others, then choosing life becomes what you *want*. In the words of Deuteronomy 30:15, we must decide to choose goodness and life instead of evil and death.

Psalm 51 is a great passage of repentance. Here, we have the words of David, a man after God's own heart. Despite his high character and series of right choices that established him as one of Israel's preeminent rulers, he made a life-altering decision to murder one of his friends so that he could steal his wife, even while he was the anointed king of Israel! At this point of conviction, David cries in verses 1 and 2.

> *Have mercy on me, O God, according to your unfailing love; according to your great compassion blot out my transgressions. Wash away all my iniquity and cleanse me from my sin.*

---

[3] Anderson, Neil T. *Victory Over the Darkness: Realize the Power of Your Identity in Christ.* Baker Publishing Group, 2020. Kindle edition. 42.

The key to David's repentance lies not only in the words David says but also in his internal realization of what he has done. His sin against others was a stab to the heart of God. David loved God. He *actually* loved God and that is why he cared that his sin stabbed God's heart. Only as David recognized his desperate need for freedom could he break the chains that kept him captive. Romans 6 teaches we were all slaves to sin, but thanks to Jesus, we can be slaves to righteousness and experience true freedom. In verse 1, Paul asks this rhetorical question: "What shall we say, then? Shall we go on sinning so that grace may increase?" He then answers this question with a second rhetorical question in verse 2, "By no means! We are those who have died to sin; how can we live in it any longer?"

If you are a slave to sin, that must be because you have not cried out as David did and totally surrendered yourself and owned the truth that you are the one who did the sinning. Until you get honest about your culpability and your total need to be saved completely by Christ, you are going to keep choosing to live in bondage.

The apostle Paul's response is one of disbelief. He asks how on earth could those who know and serve a risen Savior even consider living in willful rebellion against him? Paul then presents a powerful alternative to sinful living by his words in Romans 8, "walk in the Spirit." As we do this, we put to death the deeds of our sinful flesh and put on the nature and character of Christ. But we do not attempt to do this without asking God for help. If you try to save yourself, you won't get saved.

Part of what helps me are my wife's prayers and the intercession of the Holy Spirit, because we do not know how to pray as we should (Romans 8:26). If our prayers are honest and sincere, God takes what we offer and multiplies our prayers as Jesus did the fish and loaves.

Amanda's Prayer for Her Husband, Jim Domen

Heavenly Father,

You know our future and You know what Jim will experience today, lead my heart to pray specifically for what Jim will need today. I lean into your Holy Spirit to awaken in me what to pray right now. Search my heart and forgive me for putting my own selfish expectations onto Jim. Soften my heart with agape love for my husband, as that is what he needs today from me.

Thank you for bringing me Jim as my husband so we can do life together. I have seen him experience spiritual attack, no doubt he is on the front lines of an eternal battle as he stands for Your Truth. I speak the name of the LORD, a strong tower, to be protection for Jim. Lord, open the gates of success and favor for Jim and let him see financial success as he provides for our family. Would you give Jim a generous portion of Your wisdom as he makes decisions today?

Jim is so good at seeking counsel from trustworthy men and women. Put the right people in his life today at just the right time when he will need encouragement. Let the words I say to Jim be uplifting and my actions be loving and filling for Jim, and when I fall short would you fill in the gaps, Lord Jesus. I cannot cover all the areas Jim will need today, but You are compassionate and gracious in all these areas. Let your cleansing blood wash away all our sin and let the name of Jesus Christ be praised! In Jesus' name, Amen.

- Amanda Domen

Application

1. Can you recall the sin that catapulted you to where you are today? Was it your first viewing of pornographic material? Your first drag of a cigarette or hit of marijuana? Describe your first sin event.

    Action Item: Change your pattern. If you leave a situation and go play a video game in a location by yourself, then you find yourself going down a road that is birthing an unhealthy choice:

change the activity. Go for a walk outside instead of going online with your device.

2. If you have not confessed and repented out loud, it is necessary to do so. James 5:16 says to "confess your sins to each other and pray for each other so that you may be healed." 1 Peter 4:8 tells us that "love covers over a multitude of sins."

> **Helpful Hint**: If you are not reading this with a friend or group, who can you speak with to help you? Consider talking to a friend, pastor, mentor, or someone else you can trust, and share your confessions with them. Try online coaching at JimDomen.com

CHAPTER 2

REACH OUT TO A CHURCH

And let us consider how we may spur one another on toward love and good deeds, not giving up meeting together, as some are in the habit of doing, but encouraging one another — and all the more as you see the Day approaching.

Hebrews 10:24-25

In 2009 I worked out at LA Fitness in Yorba Linda as part of my daily routine. After finishing one of my sets, a giant of a man approached. I had seen him a few times, but always from a distance, and we had never spoken. His imposing figure signaled to me that he was not given to small chat and warm pleasantries.

At a muscular 6'5" build, he also came from an Israeli-Egyptian background and spoke in broken English. Thinking little of *this* American's need for a personal bubble, he approached me and stood some mere inches from my face.

"Are you one of those people who stand in front of people and talk about Jesus?" he demanded.

Taken aback, I smiled and replied, "Yes, I'm what they call a pastor."

The man nodded in response, but I remained unsure of his intentions. Did he hate pastors? If so, would he take a swing at me? Should I channel my inner Jackie Chan? After an awkward pause, the man introduced himself as Omar and launched into a story that nearly knocked me off my feet.

"I've been having these dreams about Jesus," he blurted. But then, as if feeling the need to clarify his statement, he said, "I don't believe in Jesus. Still, he keeps appearing to me."

Realizing my gym routine had taken an unexpected twist, I told Omar we should grab lunch so he could explain his story in detail. He agreed, and several days later we met up at a local Thai restaurant where he shared a remarkable journey that included his time as a former member of the Egyptian Special Forces. He was an assassin. He shared how his work brought him to the United States and how he now worked for the US government. With an Islamic religious upbringing, he claimed to believe in Allah.

Omar had never married. He lived in Fullerton, owned property in Victorville, and had a 16-year-old daughter who lived with her mom. He lived a comfortable life, but in recent days these visions of Jesus had turned his world upside down. They led him to question all he had ever known about life and reality.

After a fascinating two-hour conversation, I invited Omar to join me at church the next Sunday. That experience marked a change in his life.

Why Church is Important

That first Sunday, Omar sat next to me in church with great respect and homage. Dressed in a suit and tie, he stood out from the sea of casually dressed, California Christians like me with our t-shirts, jeans, and flip-flops. One look at Omar, however, and I couldn't help but be impressed.

It was clear to see that he took this decision to attend church seriously and stood in stark contrast to many Christians I knew who treated church attendance in a cavalier manner.

In a physical sense, I felt as though Omar had put on a new self. If his gym clothes represented the life he usually lived, this suit and tie represented a new identity. Like a soldier who dressed himself for a ceremony, he had prepared for this new life in Christ. That day, as I watched my new friend worship and listen with eager anticipation to the pastor's message, I couldn't help but think to myself, *this is what Jesus' Church is all about!*

I knew that church was not about a bunch of like-minded Christians getting together to perform some sort of monastic ritual. Instead, church is a place where broken, messed up people gather with the express purpose of walking in step with Christ: a place for people like Omar and me — individuals who entered a building with checkered pasts and stood in need of a Savior.

Breaking sin's grasp cannot be done on your own. It requires a community as God designed the church body. From a big-picture perspective, everyone who enters into relationship with God is connected to the universal church, the body of Christ, and the family of God, unbound by time or geographic location.[4] Jesus had His church in mind when he told the Apostle Peter in Matthew 16:18, "On this rock I will build my church, and the gates of Hades will not overcome it."

"The church is God's idea," Bishop Claude Alexander notes. "It is what Christ is building upon Himself. It is that into which God calls every person who accepts his Son by faith."[5] This universal church cannot be contained by walls made with human hands. Instead, it is a gathering of

---

4 Grudem, Wayne (2009-05-18). Systematic Theology: An Introduction to Biblical Doctrine (p. 853). Zondervan. Kindle Edition.
5 Claude Alexander, Becoming the Church, 1

saints, allowing them to worship God and minister to one-another with their unique spiritual gifts.

Within this universal church you will find countless local church congregations where believers assemble to worship God. Hebrews 10:25 (NKJV) instructs us about "not forsaking the assembling of ourselves together," thus getting at the essence of what church means: an assembly of believers, designed for the express purpose of worshiping God. Worship guides us away from unhealthy, ego-driven, mental pathways and focuses our gaze on Christ.

Through attending and engaging in a local church congregation, we position ourselves as hearers of God's Word, rather than speakers. We give our finances when we would rather hoard them. We fellowship when we might prefer to isolate. And we use our tongues to praise when we might prefer to be silent.

In corporate worship, a unique, spiritual connection takes place. While God can work through any medium – including an online service – God commands us to form a solemn assembly, so that we can together partake of the Lord's Supper, witness and perform water baptism, give each other a holy kiss, and lay hands on each other for healing. We are required to be together so that we can serve the Lord as a team, as members of one body, and do all the "one another" commandments in the Bible.

NOTE: The Holy Spirit is not confined to a church building. The Spirit goes wherever He wishes. And yet the Spirit indwells believers. In Christ, our bodies become the temple of God, so, gathering together physically is important even if forbidden by the government.

Everyone Has Something to Contribute

The beauty of God's church shines as we, a collective body, make important contributions with every member reflecting facets of God's glory and likeness like refracted light. In my coaching sessions, I emphasize that

God gives every Christian a set of spiritual gifts to share with others. 1 Corinthians 12:4-11 emphasizes this when the Apostle Paul writes:

"There are different kinds of gifts, but the same Spirit distributes them. There are different kinds of service, but the same Lord. There are different kinds of working, but in all of them and in everyone it is the same God at work. Now to each one the manifestation of the Spirit is given for the common good. To one there is given through the Spirit a message of wisdom, to another a message of knowledge by means of the same Spirit, to another faith by the same Spirit, to another gifts of healing by that one Spirit, to another miraculous powers, to another prophecy, to another distinguishing between spirits, to another speaking in different kinds of tongues, and to still another the interpretation of tongues. All these are the work of one and the same Spirit, and he distributes them to each one, just as he determines."

Personally, I have had the privilege of sitting under great teachers such as Dr. Walt Russell, former Biola University Professor at Talbot School of Theology, and a personal friend. Dr. Russell designed a *Grace Gifts Inventory Assessment*. This list of spiritual gifts includes gifts of Pastor/Teacher, Helping/Serving, Leading, Teaching, Showing Mercy, Evangelism, Administration, Giving, Faith, Exhortation, Discerning of Spirits, Apostleship, Prophecy, Miracles, Gifts of Healings, Word of Knowledge, Word of Wisdom, Speaking in Tongues, and Interpreting of Tongues.[6]

Studying this list helped me understand my areas of strength, increasing my confidence as I learned my Grace Gifts. I witnessed certain gifts and abilities in my life, such as my love for teaching and leading, and my passion for evangelism. But other gifts did not come, even supernaturally. For example, I have never spoken in tongues and would not claim to have the gift of healing. Now that I am married, I notice the way my wife's

---

6 Walt Russell, PhD, Grace-Gifts' Inventory 2011

gifts complement mine with her top gifts of helping and teaching (she homeschools our children).

Along with 1 Corinthians 12, I also value Ephesians 4:11-13 where the Apostle Paul lists the equipping gifts: "So Christ himself gave the apostles, the prophets, the evangelists, the pastors and teachers, to equip his people for works of service, so that the body of Christ may be built up until we all reach unity in the faith and in the knowledge of the Son of God and become mature, attaining to the whole measure of the fullness of Christ."

I want to highlight several important parts of this passage. First, we see that these gifts come from Christ, indicating that He gives these spiritual gifts with the intent that we will become more like Him. Second, notice the reason he gives these gifts: to build up the body and serve one another. Christ does not give spiritual gifts to showcase a believer's talents, so that they elevate themselves above others. Instead, he gives us spiritual gifts to help us serve and elevate others; to lift others up and cultivate a culture of unity. Third, spiritual gifts help us become more like Jesus. While no person can replicate the full image of God, we can better display His image as people gather and demonstrate various aspects of God's character.

Notice the reason he gives these gifts: to build up the body and serve one another.

What a wonderful demonstration of God's church, when a collective of people gather and share their gifts with one another. In so many ways, God has used a brother or sister in Christ to minister to me using their unique spiritual gifts. Maybe I needed a word of wisdom, and someone said just what I needed to hear. Or I was in pain, and God used someone who had the gift of healing.

When we gather corporately, those who have different gifts can minister to one another. For example, in certain church settings the Lord impressed on my heart, "Walk over to that person and pray with them." When I obey, amazing things happen. They often say something like, "Wow, thank you for coming over! How did you know what I was going through?" Obviously, I did not know, but the Holy Spirit did, and he worked through me to bless someone else. This only happens when I obey his prompting.

Galatians 5:16 says that "when we walk by the Spirit, we will not gratify the desires of the flesh." The Holy Spirit's work is the secret to the Christian life; he helps us walk in step with God. As we read his word, pray, and seek his face, he guides us on our journey. If you profess to follow Christ, you have the Holy Spirit at work in your life. As a result, he has equipped you with at least one spiritual gift to bless others, and very likely more than one.

> Galatians 5:16 says that "when we walk by the Spirit, we will not gratify the desires of the flesh."

When I Wanted Nothing to Do with the Church

When I was away from God, the last place I wanted to go was church. If asked why, I would mutter something like, "I don't want to be judged." Yet deep inside I knew, in truth, that I did not think people there would judge me. Instead, I feared the conviction of the Holy Spirit. I knew I was not living the way I should, and I did not want the voice of God speaking into my life.

But when I decided to get right with God, everything changed, and I turned first to the church. Coming back to the church, I found healing and restoration. I felt intense gratitude for the faithful people who helped me and the faithfulness of God I experienced within the church. In those first few months, when I came back to faith in Christ, I couldn't get enough of the Word. I sat in a church where the pastor preached strong, Biblical messages that challenged me to grow deeper in my walk with God. In fact, I loved being in church so much that I started attending three different congregations every Sunday! I hopped between three churches in Yorba Linda: Rose Drive Friends Church, Friends Church, and Calvary Chapel Saving Grace.

As I attended and engaged with other believers, God began to strip away my old way of thinking and replace it with something new. God freed me to choose life. I laid aside those desires I had for sexual encounters and decided to make God my primary pursuit. As I did this, my soul was refreshed and came alive.

God took me from "wanting nothing to do with the church" to experiencing the church as a place of healing and restoration. As this happened in the context of other believers, I made a startling discovery—I was not alone! I realized Isaiah 53:6 was right-on: "We all like sheep have gone astray." Just as I struggled with my sinful past, I found myself surrounded by others who had similar experiences. We were all broken and in need of a Savior, and we were not alone in our struggles.

It's Not About You

I faced one major challenge in coming back to church: keeping my focus on God. Loving God is very different from showing off for Him. Following Christ has nothing to do with trying to impress Him with my own acts of righteousness or with trying to make a name for myself with people in the congregation. Everything truly is about glorifying Him. Christ is glorified when we love God and love each other and do our part to defend the orphan and the widow and whoever is genuinely in need.

I want to make this important point. When I lived in a sinful relationship, so much of my life was an ego-driven *"Me. Me. Me." The autonomous self. The idolatrous self. I was my own god.* My *sexual* acts became my *primary* identity. However, when I came back to God, everything changed. Christ became my primary identity. I began to live the words of 1 Corinthians 6:19-20: *I am not my own. I was bought with a price and my life was meant to glorify God and lived out in service to Christ.*

Through my deepening relationship with God, I came to this simple, yet profound, realization: My *temptation* was not my *identity*. Words cannot express the transformative power of this concept in my life. To focus on "my temptation" was actually a subtle form of focusing on *myself*, even though I was trying to be true to God. When I turned my attention away from my temptation and onto God, I lost track of my temptation! It started to elude me. As I truly shifted my focus from self to God, I realized just how much "self" had consumed my life. Thus, I vowed to spend the rest of my life in service to God for others. As I attended church and experienced the freedom found in Christ, I started to ask the question: "Do you want to be healed?"

Your temptation is not your identity.

My life became more than just about *my* sin, and *my* personal issues. I understood I had become part of a family, and, like any good family member, I wanted to do my part to help the other members. This new freedom prompted me to seek out discipleship from others and to begin discipling others. The rewards which have flowed from a life of discipleship and disciple-making, after more than two decades of practice, have been astonishing.

> *As I truly shifted my focus from self to God, I realized just how much "self" had consumed my life.*

In Western culture, it's tempting to "want a little bit of Jesus in our lives" with the hope that he will make us a better person. We like the fact that He died for us and offers us the gift of eternal life, but we shy away from anything that seems like an obligation. The moment other people start to enter the equation and we realize that God calls us to live in communion with others, we become tempted to pull back into some form of isolation. But, as Claude Alexander notes, "You can't get Jesus without also getting his body, the church."[7]

The closer we get to Jesus and the more we love his church body, the more we realize that life is so much bigger than our little world. As Francis Chan notes, "The goal of the church is to grow up in every way into the likeness of Christ."[8]

The Church Helps You Stay in the Fight

When you set your sights on breaking sin's grasp on your life, the enemy likewise sets his sights on you. And like a shrewd tactical commander, he will work to isolate you from help, cut off your supply line of strength, and trick you into fighting the battle of your soul on *his* terms. Satan knows that *the gates of hell will not prevail* against The Church of Jesus Christ, and he will do everything in his power to separate you from the strength it offers.

---

7 Claude Alexander, Becoming the Church, 6
8 Chan, Francis (2014-01-24). The Francis Chan Collection: Crazy Love, Forgotten God, Erasing Hell, and Multiply (Kindle Locations 5981-5982). David C. Cook. Kindle Edition.

When my new friend Omar accepted Christ as his Savior and started attending church, the spiritual attacks on his soul escalated. Through countless lunches and joint workout sessions, Omar shared some incredible highs and lows. He told me of his ongoing dreams he had of Jesus, and I always left these conversations in silent awe of the way God was working in his life. But not long after Omar accepted Jesus as his Savior, his dreams began to shift from mountain-top experiences to scenes out of a horror movie. Night after night, he awoke with a sense of panic and terror as demonic oppression bombarded him with relentless assaults, attacking his new faith.

As Omar shared these horrible accounts with me, I could empathize with him. Several years earlier, after leaving my sinful lifestyle, I too had switched from a season of joy to a season of pain. Initially, I enjoyed years of bliss during the first few years after my recommitment to Jesus. I felt close to God and secure as his child. But then it seemed as though the honeymoon period ended, and wave after wave of attack rained down on my soul. At the time, it was terrifying, and I even wondered if I had done something to cause this shift. But looking back, I can now see God's faithfulness. He knew I needed extra grace those first few years, but when he saw my faith become established, He allowed my faith to be tested.

This is where the church became even more integral in my life. As I went through battles that forced me to confront the chains of my past, I leaned on the support of others. And like Omar, I came through stronger, more resilient, and more grateful for the body of Christ. At church I experienced the many attributes of the body of Christ where people come together to worship God, to seek healing, forgiveness, restoration, accountability, and growth. I do not know where I would be without the church today.

> *As we did this, the cloud over Omar's life lifted and his spirit was restored. On his own, he would have been easy picking for the enemy's advances, but through leaning on the strength of others, he could stand strong. Connecting to a church family engages this power and equips us to walk in the Spirit.*

Churches are places of community for people who are broken, in pain, and need to be restored. In his book on heaven, Randy Alcorn wrote, "A Christ-centered church is not a showcase for saints but a hospital for sinners."[9] I have found this to be true in my life. I experienced the healing, restoration and strength others offered me in my darkest hours.

I was able to offer the same kind of healing strength to Omar when he faced his own spiritual turmoil. Gradually, through linking arms in prayer together, Omar made it through his season of terror. We spent time praying together and walking through his home to pray the blood of Jesus over the doorways and rooms of his home. As we did this, the cloud over Omar's life lifted and his spirit was restored. On his own, he would have been easy picking for the enemy's advances, but through leaning on the strength of others, he could stand strong. Connecting to a church family engages this power and equips us to walk in the Spirit.

Application

1. Are you part of a church community? If so, awesome! If not, do you know how to find a biblical, local church? Start researching what men's groups are meeting at churches in your area and call some of those churches.

---

9 Alcorn, Randy (2004-10-01). Heaven (Alcorn, Randy) (Kindle Locations 940-941). Tyndale House Publishers. Kindle Edition

*Beware of churches that claim to be "progressive" on biblical morality and who are leading people astray with "woke" ideologies such as supporting abortion, gay marriage, sex confusion and sex conversion; and who elevate the dictates of government over obedience to God's written revelation in Scripture.

2. Are you part of a real men's group (a group of men who share deeply about what's going on in their lives)? For men, this is almost more important than going to a church service. It allows for male transparency and authenticity with other like-minded men. If you don't have a church men's group, your investigation from question one will be timely.

    Action Step: Breaking Sin's Grasp offers an online or retreat-style coaching program. Find out more at JimDomen.com.

CHAPTER 3

RIDE WITH OTHER MEN

Two are better than one,
because they have a good return for their labor:
If either of them falls down,
one can help the other up.
But pity anyone who falls
and has no one to help them up.
Also, if two lie down together, they will keep warm.
But how can one keep warm alone?
Though one may be overpowered,
two can defend themselves.
A cord of three strands is not quickly broken.

Ecclesiastes 4:9-12

I enjoy cycling and always have. Perhaps the roots of this athletic passion stem back to my childhood years in Tri-City Park. Those many hours of riding up and down trails with my friends planted a deep love for a sport that has endured the test of time.

I'll never forget waking up one Christmas morning when I was nine and discovering Santa had delivered the greatest Christmas gift ever — a new, 10-speed Univega mountain bike. In my excitement, I barely took time to question how Santa ever wrangled this beauty down our chimney.

Within minutes, I was out the door and riding my bike in the beautifully warm, southern California sunshine.

Although cycling was a large part of my teenage years, I pulled away from this sport as a young adult and devoted my mind to other pleasures. When I returned to God in my late twenties, I realized the need for recreational hobbies in my life. Wanting to replace my sinful past with good habits, I threw myself into work and my studies in seminary. While attempting to do a million and one good things, the combined weight of my heavy schedule began to take a toll. One of my professors noticed this and wisely suggested, "Jim, you need to do something in your life that brings you joy."

My mind immediately went to cycling. Within the week I picked up a black and yellow 56 cm Scott triathlon bike and have been riding ever since. I started competing in triathlons at age 30 and even worked my way up to a full Ironman, which includes a 2.4-mile swim, 112-mile bike ride, and 26.2-mile marathon run. Naturally, I favored the cycling part most.

My favorite aspect of cycling was riding with other guys. Men of all ages and all backgrounds joined our group. We had John the sales agent, Mike the accountant, and Dan the lawyer. Then there was me, a new returnee to the Christian faith, studying to be a pastor.

The beautiful thing about cycling is that it levels the playing field. The sport offers no favoritism to the one who makes $250,000 a year and drives a BMW. It offers no inside track to the one who earns a promotion. And it certainly won't offer you any breaks if you've had a rough day.

When cycling in a group, everyone has the same mountains to climb, the same valleys to cross. In an odd way, hill climbs remain one of my favorite terrains of the sport — but only when done in a group. Staring up at a 15% grade that seems to span to the heavens, looking at your buddies around you, and choosing to press forward generates a unique feeling of ecstasy. You know that your lungs will burn, your legs will fill with lactic acid, and your cardiovascular system will go into overdrive, but you enjoy the reward of tackling an obstacle with people you love.

And soon as you reach the summit, a new challenge emerges with the speed of a quick descent. In fact, on a typical downhill ride, it was common for our pack to reach speeds of up to 50 miles per hour. In those moments, as the wind whips through your hair and your face feels like you're having some weird form of rapid plastic surgery, every part of your being feels alive.

Riding Alone

When I committed to make cycling a part of my life again, I awoke on Saturday mornings, headed to Peet's Coffee in Irvine, California to meet up with a group of guys from Multisport Ministries (a nonprofit, triathlon men's club founded by my good friend, Eric Pace Birkholz). The group followed the Proverbs 27:17 idea of *iron sharpening iron*. Together we cycled the Santiago Canyon Loop, an aggressive 35-mile route where the weary and faint need not apply.

The topography of this path mirrored much of our lives. We all had personal peaks and valleys. Just when we felt the route was about to get easier, we encountered another hill and we'd all be off our saddles, standing on our pedals, and gasping for air until we reached the summit. A few short miles into one of these adventures and we quickly realized the importance of riding in a group.

When I'm riding by myself and the winds kick up, a forty-mile ride feels like one hundred. At times while riding in northern California, the wind speed made me feel as though I was pedaling backward! The intense headwinds felt like I had entered the eye of a hurricane. Hitting the halfway mark meant I could turn toward home, and the wind at my back could often triple my speed.

On days like these, riding alone, I found it easy to get a few miles in and wanted to give up. Sometimes I have. My desire to fight is diminished when I am alone. It's why the author of Ecclesiastes wrote these words in Ecclesiastes 4:9-10:

> Two are better than one,
> because they have a good return for their labor:
> If either of them falls down,
> one can help the other up.
> But pity anyone who falls
> and has no one to help them up.

When you ride alone, you might experience a sense of freedom. You can go anywhere you want, stop anytime you choose, and live without the limitations of other riders. But any serious rider understands the importance of a team. No Tour de France winner ever stood on the podium at the end of 23 grueling days and said, "Well, the only reason I stand here today is because of my sheer grit and determination." Instead, they point to their teammates; those other riders in their pack that made their win possible. Had it not been for the contributions of individuals on their team, the victory would not have been possible.

Life is like an extended Tour de France. Sure, you *might* be able to win a race or two on your own, but as the days turn into weeks and the weeks roll into years, you will need a team of riders around you. Just as a cord of two or three strands is not easily broken, a man with several strong friends is better able to resist the attacks of the enemy.

The headwinds a cyclist faces on a bike parallel the headwinds of life. Some days, life can be tough, and the winds of spiritual oppression, emotional baggage, and financial pressures can mix in tornado-like fashion and attack us with a vengeance. These winds are infinitely stronger than anything we might face on a 21-speed triathlon bike. These spiritual twisters can disrupt our belief in God, our view of ourselves, and how we relate to others.

When we ride through life alone, without many close relationships, we become like a stray lamb among a pack of wolves. Riding with a group provides a sense of community and empowerment; we recognize that others face the same battles we face and wrestle with similar issues.

The Benefits of Riding in Community

You can experience incredible power from riding in community with others. As a man who struggles to overcome habitual sin in his life, you need other men in your life. The primary reason for this goes back to the reality that we serve a communal God who hard-wired mankind to live in community.

For guys like me who have battled sexual sins, the need for community is more urgent and intense. Sadly, many in church communities struggle to accept individuals who don't fit inside their *typical* box.

Maybe you didn't follow my particular path of leaving a sexual lifestyle, but your choice to follow Christ will certainly come with some sort of cost. You might lose a key friendship. Family members might not look at you the same way. Those people you once thought you could count on may no longer consider you as part of their inner circle. Making the choice to follow Christ often means trading one community for another. No, I'm not talking about self-isolation. Rather, I want to address the real-life consequences that follow when we choose to deny ourselves, pick up our cross, and follow Christ daily (Luke 9:23). As we say goodbye to harmful relationships, we must say hello to some new and healthy ones.

Christian counselor Larry Crabb has written,

"A healthy community is built on friendship, on people who are committed to the art of caring engagement, an art that only the gospel makes possible in its richest form. This is what a healthy men's group should look like. It should be built on the foundation of who Jesus is and what he is doing in the lives of his followers. It should consist of men who are willing to sacrifice on behalf of others and care for one another as Christ cared for the church. When you find a group like this, it's a wonderful thing."[10]

In a world today that preaches the importance of individualism, choosing to fellowship with others becomes an antidote to the world's system. In doing so, we can sharpen and challenge one-another, and receive encouragement and motivation to keep going when life is tough. True community with other men allows us to lay down our guard and be transparent. As Gary McIntosh states, "We can choose to acknowledge our dark side, practice a life of transparency before God, and let down our guard, knowing that he will begin his refining and empowering work in us."[11]

As someone who has pastored for two decades, I've found that I must model community by example. It's not enough to tell other guys they need to pursue discipleship and seek out accountability to other men. I too must model accountability, which requires an appropriate level of transparency and vulnerability with others. It means the willingness to share my own faults and failures when it would feel more comfortable to remain silent. Leading in this manner has helped more men to do the same.

When I first started sharing my sexual past with others, I felt so much shame and embarrassment. I wondered what others would think of me. But the more I shared, the more I sensed others opening up and sharing their own struggles. It soon became clear that everybody in a church has issues—not just me! Also, the more I opened up, the more freedom I

---

10 Gladen, Steve. *Small Groups with Purpose: How to Create Healthy Communities.* (Baker Books: Ada, MI), 204. Kindle Edition
11 Gary McIntosh, Overcoming the Dark Side of Leadership, 158.

experienced. Transparency and accountability broke down walls, and I formed new friendships with other men. Choosing life means choosing to embrace accountability. Choosing accountability means being honest. Being honest makes you courageous. Being courageous is fulfilling.

If you are courageous enough to choose life, you will break free of sin's grasp!

If you are courageous enough to choose life, you will break free of sin's grasp!

Keith's Story

I've known my share of guys who have decided to ride by themselves. Such was the case with a man I'll call Keith.

A father to two children, I knew Keith as an exceptional young man and a successful business owner. After downsizing to save money, Keith's life took a turn for the worse. He said goodbye to his support structure and strong church family and developed new relationships that did NOT increase his dependence on God. At first, this seemed like a strong move for his business.

Investing their finances to grow their business, Keith, his wife and two kids moved in with friends, which proved to be a horrible mistake. Keith took a liking to one of the female housemates and developed an unhealthy relationship with her. Before long, they had an affair, and Keith's life went off the rails. Because of this decision, Keith's family has suffered years of misery, heartache, and irreparable damage.

Fortunately, I have been able to walk with Keith through this season and he regrets the decisions he made. If he could give anything to go back and make different choices, he would. But his decision to isolate and place himself in a poor environment cost him a price he will never be able to fully repay.

Like many guys his age, his problems started to compound. Keith never knew his father, so he didn't have that potentially helpful influence in his life. His relationship with his wife became strained, thus their intimacy came to a halt. Adding to these serious issues, he encountered loneliness coupled with the thrill of a new environment. It's no wonder Keith made poor choices.

Keith needed healthy male riding buddies in his life. He should never have traveled his Christian journey alone, just as you and I cannot ride alone.

Real Discipleship

When Jesus walked this earth, He rode with his own group of men, the twelve disciples. Day after day they would walk from village to village, proclaiming the good news to all who would listen. For Jesus, the essence of discipleship looked like a master and apprentice relationship. He taught his disciples to observe all he taught and did, and then replicate this pattern with others. In his closing words before his ascension into heaven, Jesus tells his followers in Matthew 28:19-20, "Therefore go and make disciples of all nations, baptizing them in the name of the Father and of the Son and of the Holy Spirit, and teaching them to obey everything I have commanded you. And surely, I am with you always, to the very end of the age."

The goal of discipleship is to become more like Christ. To this point, Jared Wilson writes, "What is discipleship, then, but following Jesus not on some religious quest to become bigger, better, or faster but to become more trusting of his mercy toward our total inability to become those things?"[12] Jesus knows we need him.

When we ride with other men and allow them to speak truth into our lives, we are following in the footsteps of Jesus' twelve disciples. We not only gain more head knowledge, but we also discover fresh ways to put our faith into action throughout the week. The process of discipleship interconnects with Christ's vision for the church. As Derwin Gray states, "Discipleship isn't just knowing more about Jesus; it's about knowing Jesus personally and being transformed into his image through constant exposure of the gospel of grace in the context of a local church."[13]

Everyone should be discipled, and everyone should disciple someone else. Unfortunately, few churches do a great job of discipling their members or even making discipleship available. As Timothy Keller observes, "Many churches do not know how to disciple members without essentially pulling them out of their vocations and inviting them to become heavily involved in church activities. In other words, Christian discipleship is interpreted as consisting largely of activities done in the evening or on the weekend."[14]

However, real discipleship does not involve simply attending a church event and saying you belong to such-and-such church in your city. Real discipleship involves getting to know the hearts of others and teaching them to obey the teachings of Jesus. This can only happen as we live life in proximity and community with others. For men like me, it might include going cycling together. But for others, it might be catching up over coffee, an early morning out on the lake, running with another man, or

---

12 Wilson, Jared C.. The Imperfect Disciple: Grace for People Who Can't Get Their Act Together. Baker Publishing Group, 2017. Kindle edition. 51.
13 Gray, Derwin L.. Building a Multiethnic Church: A Gospel Vision of Grace, Love, and Reconciliation in a Divided World. Thomas Nelson, 2021. Kindle edition. 118.
14 Keller, Timothy. Center Church: Doing Balanced, Gospel-Centered Ministry in Your City. Zondervan, 2012. Kindle edition. 175.

a night out at a sporting event. In these moments, the real value comes not just from the activity itself, but from the time spent with a friend and the meaningful and intentionally deep conversations. Get past the small talk. Ask tough questions!

As we live in close community with other men, they get to know the real us. Let's face it, at church, sometimes it feels easier to hide behind a nice facade and present an airbrushed image of ourselves. We present ourselves as men who have it all together, when deep down we deal with issues of hurt and brokenness — just like the guys in the seats around us. But through discipling others and being discipled by someone, we can experience authentic growth as the men God made us to be.

As we ride with other men, we find strength for our spiritual journey.

Discipleship is Only as Good as You Make It

Although discipleship is necessary, I offer this caveat: Discipleship is only as good as you make it. In other words, if you join a men's group but aren't willing to be a bit vulnerable and share yourself with others, don't be surprised if you don't see many benefits. Finding the right riding buddies often takes time. You might hang around a few guys one night and realize you're not a fit; maybe they have different interests than you, and you feel like an outsider. That's OK. But don't give up; keep looking. I promise there are other men who want to come alongside you and need the value of your friendship. You just need to be persistent in your search.

It has happened that I've gone out for a bike ride with a buddy and realized we probably wouldn't do it again in the future. I wanted to ride for fifty miles, whereas he just wanted a quick ride around the block without breaking a sweat. Whenever this happens, I don't give up on cycling with others. I just find another guy who is willing to go at my pace.

The same applies for discipleship. You want to surround yourself with guys who will stretch you and make you think. You don't necessarily need a collection of guys who are miles ahead of you on their spiritual journeys, but you want a variation of men who are a little bit ahead of you and a little bit less mature in their walks with God. This allows you to disciple and be discipled, mentor and be mentored, teach and be taught.

Christian psychologist Curt Thompson is right when he says, "I believe our lives will be abundant, joyful, and peaceful only to the degree that we are engaged, known, and understood by one another."[15] No, it's not always easy—especially if you're an introvert who struggles to connect with others. Make the effort, be persistent, find some riding buddies and stick together. Together you can break the grasp of habitual sin in your lives.

Application

1. Is there something in your life that you imagine, fantasize or dream about that would be destructive and not life-giving? What is it? In whom can you confide and share what's going on? Have you been riding alone? Do you need to find someone to ride with you?

    Helpful Hint: I have found it most helpful to submit myself to men whom I respect so much that I cringe at the thought of disappointing them. But it cuts to the quick when I know that I am obligated to tell men that I respect that I succumbed to temptation. Are you riding with men like this?

---

15 Thompson M.D., Curt. Anatomy of the Soul: Surprising Connections between Neuroscience and Spiritual
Practices That Can Transform Your Life and Relationships. Tyndale House Publishers, 2010. Kindle edition. Introduction.

By contrast, if I am with men who are hiding their own sins or not dealing with them, I'm not challenged by their lifestyle choices. I'm not persuded by their example and am more likely to indulge in something sinful.

CHAPTER 4

REORGANIZE YOUR SCHEDULE

There is a time for everything,
and a season for every activity under the heavens:
a time to be born and a time to die,
a time to plant and a time to uproot,
a time to kill and a time to heal,
a time to tear down and a time to build,
a time to weep and a time to laugh,
a time to mourn and a time to dance,
a time to scatter stones and a time to gather them,
a time to embrace and a time to refrain from embracing,
a time to search and a time to give up,
a time to keep and a time to throw away,
a time to tear and a time to mend,
a time to be silent and a time to speak,
a time to love and a time to hate,
a time for war and a time for peace.

Ecclesiastes 3:1-8

At times in life, we push our emotional system to the breaking point. In the summer of 1998, I lived that story. After months of international travel and working around the clock for a global-company owner, I nearly ran myself ragged. All the different time zones, weird sleep patterns, and jet lag caught up with me. I exhausted myself to the point that I could not function.

After one flight with my boss to Frankfurt Main, Germany, as we drove from the airport, it seemed as though my system simply shut down. I could barely sit up in the luxurious leather seat of his BMW 7 Series and nearly dozed off in mid-conversation. "What's the matter with you?" my boss asked. He wasn't known as the sensitive and caring type, but even he could tell something was wrong.

"I'm really tired," I said. But there was more to the story than just travel fatigue. I remember those next few days of our trip in Europe as a blur. I couldn't recall one conversation we had with a client from the next. It seemed as if someone had picked up my tiny world and shook it upside down. Everything felt off. After returning home from this trip, I told my boss I'd had enough and needed to quit.

After months of running at an unsustainable pace, I reached my limit. By this point, even the small things in life felt unmanageable and I fell into a prolonged depression. At age 23, I still had not figured out how my body worked, nor had I done the best job at implementing healthy rhythms. As a result, I stretched myself beyond my emotional, physical, and working capabilities.

During my early twenties, I often pushed my system to the breaking point. I would run full steam ahead to accomplish more and experience as many pleasures in life as possible. My rhythms were totally out of whack. I thought little about the concept of a Sabbath day of rest and worked myself into the ground, developing all sorts of unhealthy patterns. Until I realized the fruitlessness of this approach to life, I would not commit to change.

After my return to God in my late twenties, I began writing a different story. I knew from my previous failures that I had to take care of my heart, mind, soul, and strength. I started to recognize the importance of a healthy schedule. Not just a schedule that allowed me to keep on track with business meetings and professional endeavors, but one for my personal development: a schedule that helped me maintain daily rhythms. This wasn't easy at first, but little-by-little I began to adjust how I spent my days.

This process has continued to evolve. For example, 15 years after my return to God, I had a northern California pastor and colleague challenge me on my weekly rhythms. "Jim, do you take a regular Sabbath?" he asked. I hemmed and hawed, muttering something about just being in a busy season before coming clean and admitting, "No, I don't." It was embarrassing to admit. Here I was, a pastor who talked about the importance of a disciplined life, and I didn't even keep one of the basic Ten Commandments.

That day I resolved to change and to implement a weekly Sabbath time during which I could rest. Sunday didn't work for me because as a pastor, it was the busiest day of my week. I had a habit of constantly checking my phone. I didn't think I checked it that often, but my family knew I did! I decided to leave it in a separate room or to switch it off in order to focus on being present with my family. This change of pace delighted my kids. They loved having daddy present, and now my Sabbath is the favorite part of their week. Amanda even shared I was more present with her too.

Today, I've been married fifteen years, and my wife has often commented on how balanced my life has become. I run one organization and am president of another. I work hard as an author, speaker, and coach. But now I know that the most important time of my week is spent being husband to my wife and Daddy to my three kids. As the author of Ecclesiastes 3 notes, there is a season for everything. There is time to be a daddy, a husband, a leader, and a writer. These are all good things; they just need to be placed in their proper order.

Bad Systems

If you're like most people, it's all too easy to adapt to certain vices and unhealthy patterns in your life because you accepted them as normal. Maybe you drink more than you should. Or you eat out often and find yourself packing on extra pounds. Maybe you've become lazy with how you discipline your mind.

Bad systems easily come to dominate the way we live. In Christian circles, we often cast stones at people who are lazy, but we give a free pass to workaholics. We tend to condone the sin of busyness. In fact, along with overeating and indulging, busyness has become the sin-of-choice for many Christians, and many do not realize its destructive impact to their souls. In *The Ruthless Elimination of Hurry*, Jon Mark Comer writes, "Hurry and love are incompatible. All my worst moments as a father, a husband, and a pastor, even as a human being, are when I'm in a hurry." [16]

One of the most obvious ways we demonstrate a busy lifestyle is by continuously checking our phones. "Social media's algorithms are designed to feed us a never-ending loop of our desired lives, always just a handful of steps ahead of where we are—deceptively within arm's reach but always just beyond our grasp, by design." [17] As a result, Jay Kim concludes that, "The apps we use are actually using us." [18]

All my worst moments as a father, a husband, and a pastor, even as a human being, are when I'm in a hurry.

---

16 Comer, John Mark. The Ruthless Elimination of Hurry: How to Stay Emotionally Healthy and Spiritually Alive in the Chaos of the Modern World. The Crown Publishing Group, 2019. Kindle edition. 23.
17 Jay Kim, Analog Christian, 35
18 Jay Kim, Analog Christian, 8.

I've been guilty of this so many times. Maybe my name or organization is in the news, and I want to see what others are saying. I'm responding to the latest emails and worry about what this person thinks about something I've said or written. I carelessly allow the noise of this world to pull me from the people in my life that matter most.

Ultimately, the reason we develop unhealthy routines, binge-watch TV shows, obsess over sports, and fill our calendars with endless recreational hobbies is because we have bought into the lie that Christ is not enough.

When I consider the negative effects of unhealthy routines, I think of my friend Jackson as a primary case study. I first got to know Jackson while he lived in Arizona. I became his accountability partner and was quickly impressed with Jackson's commitment to purity and Christian living.

But then a higher-paying job took Jackson to the state of Tennessee. As a surgeon this move looked promising, although Jackson could not anticipate the extreme workload he would face. His move took him to Tennessee during the recovery from the COVID-19 pandemic, Jackson arrived when people were finally able and ready to have their surgical procedures completed. This meant his hours soon stretched to 14+, to 16+, and even 18-hour days.

Jackson stopped going to church, checked out on his family, avoided men's groups, and adapted to a new unhealthy way of life. With a tendency toward overworking, his job now consumed him. He started to dabble in pornography, and hook-up apps. Before long he started to sleep around for the first time in his life.

Without question, tremendous heart and emotional issues played out in Jackson's life. After his dramatic decline, his unhealthy routines became evident and played a large role in his spiritual collapse. When he felt tired and lonely and needed something to take the stress off, instead of scaling back and recommitting to his time with God, he doubled down on unhealthy habits, using porn and sex to offer him some relief. In short,

Jackson had a lot of good head knowledge, but he lacked the key disciplines that establish a healthy spiritual life.

Thankfully, after several talks and tough accountability discussions, he realized the error in his ways and began to reorganize his schedule.

Key Disciplines

One key to a healthy schedule is making steadfast commitments to action that trigger your ability to do the right thing.

Several years ago, I flew to the U.S. Capitol along with several other pastors and had the opportunity to invite Nebraska's United States Senator Ben Sasse to speak to 157 California pastors in Washington, D.C. through ChurchUnited.com. I respected Senator Sasse for his Christ-like walk and many of the pastors in attendance thought he should run for president of the United States. However, something he said only heightened my admiration. One of the pastors asked him how he remained faithful to his wife, considering he lived in a D.C. culture that made extramarital affairs common. Senator Sasse responded by sharing that he never traveled by himself; he was always with his wife or one of his kids. This action step made it far less likely he would slip into sin.

Since that exchange, I've done my best to follow this advice. I almost never travel alone and either take a family member or accountability partner with me. This keeps me on track and helps me avoid foolish decisions.

Another way I've disciplined myself is to guard against busyness. Unfortunately, we tend to excuse the sin of busyness, with many of us buying into the cultural narrative and a skewed work ethic which says, "working more is better." How many times have you asked someone, "How are you doing?" and they respond with "I'm busy." Busyness keeps us from addressing our issues. Intentionally reorganizing our schedules means eliminating busyness by ridding our lives of unproductive things. To do more, you must do less.

Healthy routines and quality sleep are important. For me, this means maintaining certain disciplines, such as putting my device in another room and giving my body the rest it needs to recharge, away from distractions. Make it your goal to pre-plan your routines and implement them. Maybe this means getting up at 6 AM, going to the gym, having breakfast, and then heading off to work. A disciplined life has tremendous value.

Whatever your routine looks like, build it in such a way that you replace old habits. Maybe you are tired at the end of the day. Maybe it is during your regular breaktime. Look at your schedule and identify key times you act out and do things you shouldn't. Your new routine needs to replace this time and behavior with something new and healthy, such as a phone call to a Christian friend. If you're married, take your wife out for a walk, do an activity with her, rather than be alone. Pour into your children rather than into yourself. Replace self-centered habits with good habits that include others.

A couple of questions you should ask yourself include: Am I keeping a regular Sabbath day of rest? Do I have a habitual form of exercise I enjoy? Am I volunteering my time? Am I engaged each week in my church? What does my prayer life look like? Do I read God's Word every day? Am I listening to music and watching entertainment that edifies my soul?

The joys of a strong spiritual life only come as we embrace the value of a disciplined life.

The Insanity Cycle

It's often said the definition of insanity is doing the same thing over and over and expecting a different result.

In 2004, I experienced a breakthrough moment in my life, during my first semester in seminary pursuing a Master of Divinity. While in a cohort of youth pastors also in seminary, one morning our professor, Stephen Peisner, PhD, led the class in a Timeline Experience. He gave each of us twenty minutes alone to reflect and create a timeline of our lives. On this timeline, we listed any significant events. Then we organized them on the timeline according to their dates.

I started to make my list: graduation from high school, my first job, and my years wandering away from God. When all was said and done, I probably had thirty items on the timeline. Dr. Peisner then called the class to reassemble, and he told us to look at what we had just written. In particular, he wanted us to notice observable patterns in our lives.

To my shock, I instantly knew why he wanted us to complete this exercise. When I looked at the timeline, I saw my life patterns and they were repeating. My life had become the definition of insanity! I vowed that day to change things. I took steps to reorganize my life so I would NOT repeat the same patterns.

The more I reflected on this exercise, the more I could sympathize with the children of Israel who wandered in the desert for over forty years, seemingly making the same mistakes over and over. Clearly, human nature defaults to repeating the same mistakes.

I had observed this during my time in Al-Anon, a public support group for codependent people (Alcoholics Anonymous is for addicts). How many times would I see a fellow member come in who had been verbally, physically, or emotionally abused by a partner (the addict). Though in most cases the people being abused could choose to leave their abusers, they often chose to stay. It was as if they had grown comfortable with the predictability an abusive relationship would offer. Despite being in an abusive relationship with another man, I too had chosen to stay in the hopes that things would change. My eyes were opened during my third

Al-Anon meeting. I saw how codependent people were like me! I decided to change and leave my abuser.

From Stripper to Saint

The insanity cycle can catch up with anyone, taking them down a path they might not have imagined. A father's abuse led to his reaction of becoming a stripper and his schedule was shattered. Such was the case with my friend Jim Sumner, who I asked to share the following story.

> By the time I graduated high school, my identity was set: I was stupid, ugly, and insignificant. No award bestowed on me by teachers, coaches, or peers could convince me otherwise. I was a victim of my circumstances. The dynamics in my family and the environment at my school were riddled with ridicule, rejection, unresolved conflict, criticism, disrespect and void of encouragement and love. The damaging effects of my deprived life bequeathed to me a disintegrated self.
>
> For the next nineteen years my primary goal was to escape the shame that came with having to be myself. I used humor, booze, TV, drugs, and legally changed my last name because being Jim "Czmowski" meant I was "a stupid Polack," a scapegoat to be jeered at, a target for a "real man" to mock. Though I wanted to perform as an actor, I ended up being a dancer, and my stage name covered up my changed name which gave me a double covering. Ironically, I hid on stage by stripping. I went from being a virgin who was prom king to being a fornicator and adulterer, and yet intimacy was the thing that I avoided most successfully. The next thing you know, I had a one-night stand with a woman who wanted to marry my false self.
>
> In 1994, I fell into the web of a fatal attraction. The woman lived out-of-state and was a friend of my friend's friend, and

over the course of about a year, I hooked up with her three times. Little did I know that she herself was a shattered individual. She had an unfathered daughter from her teenage years and a desperate desire to be rescued from the biting disappointment of being jilted by her child's father, ignored by her own father, and abused by her stepfather. When she realized I was there for my own pleasure, not her future, her turmoil exploded into rage. All her ire against men who had abandoned her consumed her with a thirst for revenge.

On October 19, 1994, I was arrested on the false charges of first-degree rape and first-degree assault and found myself locked up in maximum security at Cook County Correctional Facility in Chicago, Illinois, the most dangerous jail in the country. No betrayal in my life had been more threatening than the venomous lie told by the woman who wanted me and had phoned me tirelessly just to hear my voice. The first evening at Cook County, two jailhouse inmates distorted my words and demanded to meet up with me in the morning. Secured by the evening lockdown, I finally felt a moment of reprieve, only to be ambushed by my cellmate – my "celly" – who accosted me not with violence, but rather with loud cries of hellfire and brimstone. 'Confess your sins!' he yelped, as I worried about being the roomie of a Jesus freak. Motivated by nothing but sheer self-preservation, I decided to pray a phony prayer.

My two-minute intent of confessing a few lies morphed into unprecedented remorse. Two hours' worth of coughing up crud and wickedness discharging from my heart of stone was followed by God giving me a heart of flesh. Tears streamed down my cheeks as the Spirit of God opened my eyes, not only to my transgressions, but also to the grace of a very, very different kind of Father. My celly said God would forgive me if I asked. Amazed, I made the ask and felt the miracle of being unloaded from the heaviness of my sin that I had lugged around for decades in denial. The song Amazing Grace provides lyrics that explain my experience: "Amazing grace how sweet the sound that saved a wretch like me. I once was lost, but now am found. Was blind, but now I see!" Ironically, I sat imprisoned unjustly for that which I *was not* guilty of and discovered *what* I was guilty of. In confinement I found freedom because in that cold, stark jail cell, God enveloped me with the warmth of the love of Jesus.

When my case came to court and the judge saw the evidence, God opened the door for me to share in open court that I had experienced the marvel of the joy of salvation. "I forgive you," I said to my accuser. Being released from the charges was a monumental relief, but it paled in comparison to the rest and restoration that God gave me in Christ, who died for me sacrificially. I encountered God. I wasn't saved by an evangelistic formula. I was saved by coming to terms with my real self and seeing my total need to be delivered. I found myself when God found me. That is just the beginning of my story. As for the woman and her daughter and my cellmate, I want them and everyone else to meet and experience God too.

Notice how this all started. Jim believed a narrative that said he was "stupid, ugly, and insignificant." The powers of darkness then used that belief to lead Jim into a series of devastating choices. He ended up living a lifestyle he would have never imagined and sank to a place he never thought he'd go. But when God stepped into his life, everything changed. Now, Jim is someone whose schedule couldn't look more different today. He has a wonderful wife, loves Jesus, and makes decisions that would shock anyone who knew him in his previous life.

Sarah's Prayer for Her Husband, Jim Sumner

At age thirteen, I began to pray for my future husband, not knowing that it would be twenty years from then until I married him, and certainly not knowing that when he was thirty-seven, he would have a Saul-Paul conversion. What blows me away is that I got to participate in praying for Jim's conversion.

Over the years as Jim's wife, I have prayed: Dear Lord, thank You so much for Jim. Thank You for how handsome he is and cute in his personality and funny and witty and helpful – he does so many chores. Thank You that he forgives me and participates with such zeal in serving You. Thank you for the example he sets in being so considerate of others. Please help him every day to keep pace with the Holy Spirit, to listen to You and trust You and love You with all his heart, mind, soul and strength. Please help him to respond with wisdom in conversations. I pray for him to be quick to hear, slow to speak, and slow to anger. Please help him to be gentle and kind. I pray fervently for him to cast all his anxiety on You. Please help Jim to remember the joy of his salvation and serve as a bold witness to our neighbors. Please help him to slow down and ask good questions. Please heal him from past shame and make him sexually pure. I pray that You would ambush him and speak to him the moment that he begins to fall astray. Please help him to be vulnerable, so comforted by Your Spirit. I pray this in Jesus' Name, Amen

-Sarah Sumner, MBA, PhD

Develop Your Own System

As an interesting side note, Jim Sumner's wife, Sarah, has had a tremendous impact on my life. I first met her when she was my professor at Azusa Pacific University back in the early 2000s. But since then, I have benefited from services at Right On Mission (rightonmission.org), the organization she founded and now leads. Right On Mission is both an online seminary and consulting firm, specializing in teaching Christians how to live on mission, and not veer off mission. In one unhurried session with Dr. Sarah Sumner, MBA, PhD, she can figure out and articulate your purpose. All at once, they can write your mission statement, vision statement, and why statement (and do the same for your nonprofit or church). I gained so much clarity by receiving my life mission statement: *"To urge men to choose life."* When men choose life, they become better men. Choosing life, not death (Deuteronomy 30:15-19), structurally transforms men into better sons, brothers, husbands and fathers, and sets them up to walk in greater freedom.

But now, listen to my individual Why Statement: *"I believe when men respect their constant need for help, God incarnates them to be invincible."* Do you hear what that statement says? As men, we must respect—not just accept, but respect—our constant need for help. When we get that help, the constant help we need, we can break sin's grasp. Because I truly believe that I pursued help. I received help. I got help. And again, I have to tell you how that "constant help" has freed me to do what the world says is impossible. I have *not* acted out physically on sinful sexual urges ever since I started getting the kind of help I needed.

The battle has moved from acting out physically to battling in my mind. God's help through His Spirit, His Word, His people can elevate you above your sinful *"stuckness."* I really do believe that when men, such as Keith who had an affair with a housemate, and Hunter who lost his youth job at the church, learn to respect their need for constant help, they can do what seemed impossible for them. After living as a gay man, I thought it was impossible for me to feel attracted to a woman. I never thought I would have kids of my own with a beautiful wife I truly loved. I never thought I could walk in holiness until I respected my constant need for help. I didn't think I could serve as a pastor or a global ministry leader. This realization of needing help from men <u>and from women</u> has given greater insight to why God created women to "help" men as helpmates, and win the war in which we are engaged.

> *I believe when men respect their constant need for help,
> God incarnates them to be invincible.*

You will not stay in the grasp of sin if you decide to respect your constant need for help. You will grow. You will fly. It's basically up to you: Do you want to be free? The way to enter freedom is by choosing to be helped. To get the right kind of help is to choose life.

Because I value how I spend my days, I have looked for help from other leaders as well, such as Franklin Covey, and a Christian named Bob Shank (who founded The Master's Program at priorityliving.org). Their help was valuable, and yet honestly nothing quite worked for me, regarding finding my own rhythm in daily living out of the reach of sin's grasp, until I developed my own system. I'm not one of those productivity gurus you'll see on YouTube, but I do adhere to these basics.

For starters, any event I schedule goes on my digital calendar. I also invite my wife to the event if it involves her or the kids. Similarly, I invite others on my work team to events that involve them. Although a digital calendar is non-verbal, it is a great way to communicate and inform those whom you desire to keep informed.

Finding a rhythm that works for you takes time and involves a lot of trial and error. For example, my wife Amanda discovered that whenever our family goes on a trip, we need a full day before the trip to prepare and a full day afterward to decompress. Otherwise, we become stressed! She's always had this wonderful sensitivity to our family members and dynamics, so it is easy for her to adjust accordingly. It took time for me to come along, but it alleviates stress and makes traveling kinder and nicer for her and our children.

Reorganizing your schedule doesn't solve every problem you face, but it sure helps. It's often been said (including by my grandma) that an idle mind is the devil's workshop. When you know why and how you're going to spend your time, you're much less prone to fall into the traps the enemy sets for you.

Develop your own system. You'll likely need help in doing that.

Application

1. Albert Einstein's definition of insanity is "doing the same thing over and over and expecting a different result." How do you stop insanity? Change the routine! What about your routine needs to be changed?

2. What needs to happen for you to reorganize your schedule? What will your new schedule look like? Don't delay; create it!

CHAPTER 5

REPLACE BAD HABITS

> Therefore, if anyone is in Christ, the new creation has come: The old has gone, the new is here! All this is from God, who reconciled us to himself through Christ and gave us the ministry of reconciliation: that God was reconciling the world to himself in Christ, not counting people's sins against them. And he has committed to us the message of reconciliation. We are therefore Christ's ambassadors, as though God were making his appeal through us. We implore you on Christ's behalf: Be reconciled to God. God made him who had no sin to be sin for us, so that in him we might become the righteousness of God.
>
> 2 Corinthians 5:17-21

In 2019, I traveled to Taipei, Taiwan in my role as the President of the Global Rainbow Crossers Alliance for our international summit. A Rainbow Crosser is someone who was formerly LGBTQ+ and has "crossed over" to the true rainbow of God's truth and promises. After one of the main sessions of hearing a speaker at that conference, I stopped at a booth manned by a guy named Jesús Carbonell who stood next to his table in front of a three-foot-long picture of a physically fit, strikingly beautiful woman. Assuming she was his wife, I asked him how long he had been married. That's when those around me started to chuckle.

Taking my question in stride, Jesús looked at me and said, "That's not my wife. That was *me* during my years as a transgender female!"

My mouth gaped in amazement at the drastic contrast. Here stood Jesús in front of me with short, cropped hair and a dark brown beard, next to a picture of what appeared to be a woman with long hair and a smooth face. As if he could sense the question that I was about to ask, Jesús offered a timely explanation. "The reason I have this picture is to remind myself and others of the person I used to be."

In my first book, *Not a Mistake*, I asked Jesús to share his transformation story. Jesús' story is so encouraging because he reminds us that anyone can change. Anyone in Christ can put off the old and put on the new. Anyone who seeks God can be transformed from who they used to be. By choosing life, any person can miraculously be made new, with a brand-new identity found in Christ.

When I travel, I frequently carry a large three-foot by two-foot poster-sized picture of my wife and family. I do this because many people treat me as though my life's story is just a mistake. Whenever I tell them about my past, how I once lived in a gay relationship, and now have a wife and three kids, their eyes widen due to shock. Only a few have dared ask me the questions that I know many have wondered silently. *Is Jim sexually attracted to men? If so, doesn't this mean he is gay? How could he ever have a wife and three kids? Isn't he just living a lie? Isn't he denying who he really is?*

By choosing life, any person can miraculously be made new, with a brand-new identity found in Christ.

Ignoring the obvious air of condescension, I can't help but have a sense of true compassion for those who ask these types of unspoken questions. Many people have been trained their entire lives, even brainwashed to believe that if someone like me is attracted to someone else of the same-sex, the only way we can be true to ourselves is to pursue same-sex relationships. They view sexual identity as one's only identity. They believe that people like me must have ulterior motives. They don't trust us because by default they think that we are obviously living a lie. To them, men and women like me cannot exist.

This is where I am thankful for passages of Scripture like 2 Corinthians 5:17: "Therefore, if anyone is in Christ, the new creation has come: The old has gone, the new is here!"[19]

Putting off the Old Self

Despite knowing that our true identity is found in God, a spiritual war takes place inside our minds. The Apostle Paul talked about this in Romans 7. In verses 18-19, he writes, "For I know that good itself does not dwell in me, that is, in my sinful nature. For I have the desire to do what is good, but I cannot carry it out. For I do not do the good I want to do, but the evil I do not want to do—this I keep on doing." This passage speaks to the battle that often rages in people's lives today. They want to do what is good and put off their old selves, but there is this constant tug to do what is evil. To this struggle believers face, Dane Ortlund makes this observation:

"The battle of the Christian life is to bring your own heart into alignment with Christ's, that is, getting up each morning and replacing your natural orphan mindset with a mindset of full and free adoption into the family of God through the work of Christ…, who loved you and gave himself for you out of the overflowing fullness of his gracious heart."[20]

Every morning we wake up with a choice: to walk in our old ways, or to walk in the newness of life we find in Christ. Every child of God must

---

19 Jim Domen, *Not a Mistake*, 210-212
20 Dane C. Ortlund, *Gentle and Lowly: The Heart of Christ for Sinners and Sufferers*. Crossway, 2020. Kindle edition. 181.

make this conscious decision: the minute-by-minute decision to walk as Christ walked and live as he would want us to live.

While many believers are quick to focus on Romans 7— "For I do not do the good I want to do, but the evil I do not want to do – this – I keep on doing."—and hold it up as the norm for a believer, the real norm for followers of Christ should be found in all of Romans 6, 7 and 8. Consider these words in Romans 8:1-2: "Therefore, there is now no condemnation for those who are in Christ Jesus, because through Christ Jesus the law of the Spirit who gives life has set you free from the law of sin and death."

The first four verses of Romans 6 are even stronger, making it abundantly clear what Paul thinks about the idea of living a life of sin:

> What shall we say, then? Shall we go on sinning so that grace may increase? By no means! We are those who have died to sin; how can we live in it any longer? Or don't you know that all of us who were baptized into Christ Jesus were baptized into his death? We were therefore buried with him through baptism into death in order that, just as Christ was raised from the dead through the glory of the Father, we too may live a new life."

To Paul, the idea of continuing in sin was appalling. How could one even conceive to understand who Jesus is, what he has done, and then make choices to willfully walk against him? As Paul wrote to the Ephesians, "For you were once darkness, but now you are light in the Lord. Live as children of light." (Ephesians 5:8). First John 3:10 is also clear, "This is how we know who the children of God are and who the children of the devil are: Anyone who does not do what is right is not God's child."

Putting on the New Self

Part of this replacement process of putting on our new selves is what the Bible calls sanctification. Wayne Grudem wrote, "Sanctification is a progressive work of God and man that makes us more and more free from sin and like Christ in our actual lives."[21] Far from being an instant act, sanctification is a lengthy process only to be completed when we see Jesus face-to-face (I Corinthians 13:12).

In everything we do, God is in the process of chipping away at our selfishness, pride, and insecurities in order to fill us with his holy character. Speaking to this process, Walter Henrichsen wrote, "God sets about to systematically destroy our worldly hope, replacing it with a purified hope, a 'hope that does not disappoint us.' ... As God brings you through the process of sanctification, he will strip you of all impure hope. More often than not, you will find this painful as you experience defeat and unfulfilled dreams."[22]

The Apostle Paul puts it this way in Ephesians 4:22-24: "You were taught, with regard to your former way of life, to put off your old self, which is being corrupted by its deceitful desires; to be made new in the attitude of your minds; and to put on the new self, created to be like God in true righteousness and holiness."

We all must wrestle with the ongoing challenge: *How do I put off my old self?* In response, we can ask ourselves three questions.

1. *What was I like before I knew Jesus?*
2. *Which of my behaviors brought me to destruction physically, emotionally, mentally, or spiritually?*
3. *How will I work now to aggressively put on my new self and walk with Christ as my primary identity?*

---

[21] Wayne Grudem, (2009-05-18). *Systematic Theology: An Introduction to Biblical Doctrine* (p. 746). Zondervan. Kindle Edition.
[22] Walter A. Henrichsen, *Thoughts from the Diary of a Desperate Man: A Daily Devotional* (El Cajon, CA: Leadership Foundation, 2011), 308.

I found my "new self" by capturing a bigger vision for my life. For me, it wasn't enough to say, *I'm not going to pursue a sexual lifestyle.* I had to replace this "old" way of living by making new friends and establishing healthy male relationships. To this point, author Mark Batterson writes, "You don't overcome sin by focusing on not sinning. You need a dream that is bigger and better than the temptations you're trying to overcome. You need a dream that doesn't allow you to become spiritually sidetracked, a dream that demands your utmost for His highest."[23]

If you're trying to break free from the grasp of sin, you need not only to *stop* doing habitual sinful behaviors, but you also need to *start* making habitual good choices. If part of your old lifestyle included visiting a certain strip club on the weekdays, you might need to take a different route home from work. If part of your old life was an addiction to pornography, you might need to cancel your cable subscription or get radical and exchange your smartphone for a dumb one!

Putting off the old self and putting on the new involves a series of strategic, habitual decisions to walk in all the light God gives us.

Helpful Hint: You likely won't find it too hard to identify your primary issues. This is probably one reason you're reading this book. Ask yourself this key question every day: *How am I going to put on the new self and live in the new self?*

Putting off the old self and putting on the new involves a series of strategic, habitual decisions to walk in all the light God gives us.

---

23 https://www.markbatterson.com/no-guts-no-glory/

Temptation Doesn't Define You

Your temptation is not "Who" you are. It's critically important as you understand sin habits, they are not your identity! I cannot emphasize enough how separating your temptation from who you are in Christ will aid in breaking your sinful choices. It's so easy to define ourselves by our failures and shortcomings instead of looking at who we are in Christ. This concept will aid in reestablishing healthy habits guiding you to victory.

The Science of Habits

The process of forming new habits has a profound ripple effect on our lives. One poor habit can result in a series of wrong decisions. But one good habit can reap a harvest of good results. In *Atomic Habits*, James Clear writes:

"Habits are the compound interest of self-improvement. The same way that money multiplies through compound interest, the effects of your habits multiply as you repeat them. They seem to make little difference on any given day and yet the impact they deliver over the months and years can be enormous. It is only when looking back two, five, or perhaps ten years later that the value of good habits and the cost of bad ones becomes strikingly apparent."[24]

Thinking about habits like compound interest has a way of keeping us on point. We often think of the price we pay for negative habits, but we should also note the price we pay for *not* establishing positive ones. Each year that passes without positive habits established is like potential compound interest flushed down the drain.

We can anchor our understanding about the brain's process of forming healthy habits in science. Much has been written about the ways our

---

24 James Clear, Atomic Habits: An Easy & Proven Way to Build Good Habits & Break Bad Ones. Penguin Publishing Group, 2018. Kindle edition. 16.

minds form mental habits. Concerning these habits, Dr. Daniel Amen makes this fascinating observation:

"When neurons fire together, they wire together, through a process called long-term potentiation (LTP), and habits and responses become an ingrained part of your life. LTP occurs when the brain learns something new, whether it's good or bad, and causes networks of brain cells to make new connections. Early in the learning process, the connections are weak, but over time, as behaviors are repeated, the networks become stronger, making the behaviors more likely to become automatic, reflexive, or habitual. At this point, the networks are said to be "potentiated."[25]

Amen's statement helps us understand the importance of strengthening those neural pathways in our brains. It's a bit like a rut. For example, if you visit various spots along the famous Oregon Trail, you'll notice a set of wagon-wheel-sized ruts that are clearly visible for the eye to see. Even though it has been over a hundred years since this trail was in major use, the thousands of travelers who used this route formed a deep path that remains today.

Forming habits in our brains is like forming a trail. When we make a series of right decisions day after day, new neural pathway "ruts" are formed in our brains. The key, though, is to change our habits in the right way.

Implement the 21/90 Rule

Habit coaches often talk about the 21/90 Rule. It goes like this. *You commit to a certain action for 21 days and work at it every day.* By the three-week mark, this new routine will start to feel like a habit. The goal then is to keep at it until the 90-day mark. By this point, this new action should be a natural part of your daily routine.

---

25 https://www.amenclinics.com/blog/7-ways-to-use-your-brain-to-change-any-habit-even-really-bad-ones/

REPLACE BAD HABITS

Building great habits isn't rocket science. It just takes daily discipline to do the right thing, day after day. The key to forming good habits is making good decisions. One of the best questions you can ask yourself all throughout the day is this: *"Will this action help me get where I want to go?"* Are you on a diet, but you feel like you want a cheeseburger at In-n-Out? Ask yourself, *"Will going to In-n-Out help me achieve my goals?"*

If that doesn't work, insert a person into the mix. Think of someone you admire and when you feel tempted to give in or quit, ask yourself, *"What would this person do?"* Would they give in, or would they press forward? Would they renege on a commitment they have made to themselves and others, or would they keep their word?

As you start making good choices, you are well on your way to a new life. But this new way of living should come with a warning. In Matthew 12:43-45, Jesus makes this seemingly bizarre statement concerning demons:

> When an impure spirit comes out of a person, it goes through arid places seeking rest and does not find it. Then it says, 'I will return to the house I left.' When it arrives, it finds the house unoccupied, swept clean and put in order. Then it goes and takes with it seven other spirits more wicked than itself, and they go in and live there. And the final condition of that person is worse than the first. That is how it will be with this wicked generation.

Among the numerous applications we can derive from this passage, it teaches us a primary lesson about the danger of relapse. When Jesus does his work in our lives and sweeps our spiritual houses clean, we must take care never to invite or allow the enemy of our souls to regain a foothold in our lives. If he does, he will come back *seven-times stronger* (according to Jesus) and look to take more control of our lives.

The danger of relapse is the reason why groups such as Alcoholics Anonymous caution their members against speaking prematurely about their personal experiences coming out of their addictions, and instead refer to themselves as recovering addicts. They do this because the power of addiction is strong, and aside from a transformative move of God, most former addicts will always struggle with their flesh to war against the temptation that once held them captive.

This realization should make us approach the act of habit-forming with a degree of humility and focus. We must get the bad stuff out of our lives. That's step one. But then we must intentionally replace our bad habits with a lifegiving variety of good habits, disciplines, activities and relationships.

Make a Declaration

Although this book speaks about habits and addictions, I should confess, I've never had a drug or substance-abuse addiction. I started chewing tobacco in college but usually only did it while I hunted. I've tried everything from Red Man Indian long chew, Snuff, Skoal, and Copenhagen to pouch tobacco.

I started smoking cigarettes when I was in my early 20's. Why? Because society told me I shouldn't, and I wanted to be a rebel. I did it precisely because I wasn't supposed to do it. Yes, I know that wasn't wise—it was illogical, but to me all the cool people always stood outside of the building and smoked cigarettes (vaping and e-cigarettes had not been invented, and Hookah was still a practice primarily in the Middle East).

By 2002 I had smoked cigarettes for about four years. I smoked about a pack a day of Marlboro Lights. I tried a few other brands, like Natural American Spirit (Indian cigarettes), that really packed a punch with an herbal natural flavor. But if I really wanted a buzz, I'd smoke a Marlboro Red, loaded with nicotine.

In my proud defiance, I even tried "girl cigarettes," thin, feminine-feeling, menthol smokes. They were girly with an alcohol burn that kicked in after a few puffs. The point is, I would smoke anything! That's how cool I was.

Then I decided I wanted to make a change and wean myself off cigarettes. It was January in Palm Springs when I decided to try the patch. The NicoDerm patch was time-released and helped mitigate cravings by releasing nicotine via the skin over a 24-hour period. I'd never tried a patch before, but it sounded easy enough. However, that's when I tried something I should have never attempted: I decided to smoke while wearing the patch. At the time, I was alone in North Palm Springs at the art gallery that my business partner and I owned. I decided to leave the main gallery area for a few quick drags.

Stepping out of the hot California sun and back into the cool air-conditioned room, I suddenly felt a blast of heat flash like lightning through my body. My internal temperature skyrocketed, and I felt like I was on fire. The cool room was no match for the fire that was raging inside. My heart rate began to race so uncontrollably that I thought my heart was going to leap out of my chest. I was shaking and couldn't stand up straight. I should have called 9-1-1 but instead I called my business partner. After telling him what happened, he said he'd show up with a cure. He brought over some type of juice that helped counteract the nicotine punch that had been dealt to my system. Several hours later, I was back to normal.

After that close call, I ditched the patch for several months and began chain smoking once again. Finally, in April of that same year, I made the decision. I told my business partner, "I'm stopping smoking," and that day I quit — cold turkey. Notice the vernacular I used. I did not say, "I'm *going* to stop smoking," or "I'm going to *try* to stop smoking." I decided and declared in that moment, "I'm stopping smoking!"

Words are powerful. They have meaning. When it comes to establishing new habits, it's easy to make well-intentioned statements. Here are some examples of wishful thinking that will not lead to change:

"One day I'm going to quit drinking so much."

"Soon, I'm going to quit maxing out my credit cards."

"I want to quit my porn habit."

Real change occurs when we move from wishful thinking into declarative action. We make a solid commitment and stick with the decision we have made.

Real change occurs when we move from wishful thinking into declarative action.

Five months after making that decisive declaration, I sat on a Laguna Beach balcony at my buddy's home, looking out over the Pacific Ocean. As he sat there smoking and exhaling puffs of smoke, I suddenly felt the urge to take a drag.

"Hey, let me bum a cigarette," I said.

He handed me a Marlboro Light. I took three puffs, and then it was as if I caught myself. This was not the path I wanted to take. I knew what it was like to experience freedom from this habit, and there was no way I was going to go back.

Today, the only urge I want to have is "to urge men to choose life." I reject urges that are sinful. Ever since that day over twenty years ago, I have not taken another puff of a cigarette.

The Power of Great Habits

You will gain tremendous benefits and strength from discarding poor habits, such as smoking, by forming better habits to take their place. Habits—both good and bad—are patterned and predictable and they can be changed. Social psychologist and author, Dr. Amy Johnson, wrote *The Little Book of Big Change* (2016, New Harbinger Publications). As a guest on Dr. Caroline Leaf's podcast, she said, "Your brain is like a machine; it is demanding that you do something or act in a certain way because it has been conditioned by your behavior… Overcoming a bad habit or addiction is not about making something go away or stop. It is about learning how to be free of the urges to act or think in a certain a way, separating yourself from them."[26]

We can either form poor habits or good habits. The choice is up to us. We get to choose. According to James Clear, "The holy grail of habit change is not a single one-percent improvement, but a thousand of them."[27] It's choosing to make right decisions when we wake up, how we speak to our family, what we do at work, and how we spend our evenings. And for those times we mess up, we lean on God's grace, and get back on track. Max Lucado puts it this way:

> "Grace is God as heart surgeon, cracking open your chest, removing your heart—poisoned as it is with pride and pain—and replacing it with his own. Rather than tell you to change, he creates the change. Do you clean up so he can accept you?

---

[26] https://drleaf.com/blogs/news/how-to-unwire-addiction-toxic-habits-from-our-brains-why-focusing-on-willpower-is-ineffective-and-counterproductive-tips-on-how-to-help-someone-without-enabling-them-with-dr-amy-johnson. September 27, 2020
[27] James Clear, Atomic Habits: An Easy & Proven Way to Build Good Habits & Break Bad Ones. Penguin Publishing Group, 2018. Kindle edition. 251.

No, he accepts you and begins cleaning you up. His dream isn't just to get you into heaven but to get heaven into you."[28]

That is what God is doing in our lives. With each habitual change we make to put off our old selves and put on the new character of Christ, we reflect more of the heavenly nature of Christ to those around us.

Application

Helpful Hint: The key to effective habitual change is identifying those things in our lives we need to change and then coming up with a workable plan that will make our new goals become a reality.

1. Make a list of three habits or behaviors you need to change. Next to each one, write a new goal along with a few practical steps you can take today to achieve it.

2. Do you know a man who has established strong habits in his life? Pray and ask him if he'd be willing to journey with you as you begin transforming your life and walking in the light.

Helpful Hint: How can you put off the old self? Identify your old self and put on your new self, clothed in righteousness (Romans 13:14, 2 Corinthians 5:21, 1 Peter 2:24). Then put on the full armor of God, daily (Ephesians 6:10-18).

---

[28] Lucado, Max (2012-09-11). *Grace: More Than We Deserve, Greater Than We Imagine* (p. 10). Thomas Nelson. Kindle Edition.

CHAPTER 6

RETRAIN YOUR BRAIN

Therefore, I urge you, brothers and sisters, in view of God's mercy, to offer your bodies as a living sacrifice, holy and pleasing to God—this is your true and proper worship. Do not conform to the pattern of this world, but be transformed by the renewing of your mind. Then you will be able to test and approve what God's will is—his good, pleasing and perfect will.

Romans 12:1-2

"I want to help you avoid a catastrophe." Orthopedic surgeon and longevity physician, Dr. Mark Legome, shared sternly with me during my appointment. Not once did I ever envision those seven words being used to project a grim forecast of my trending health status.

It was April of 2022. My wife and I sat in my doctor's office in Mission Viejo, California as he poured over twelve pages of my bloodwork details. The mood was somber.

"Jim, you're a borderline diabetic," the doctor began. "You are dehydrated and have artery blockage, low testosterone, an unhealthy metabolism, an enlarged prostate, and a virus in your brain."

As if pausing for effect before continuing, he added. "Oh, and you have gout, sleep apnea, a possible pituitary tumor, high blood pressure, possible kidney issues and all the genetic markings of multiple sclerosis. And just for good measure," he added, "you also have a gut yeast (fungal) infection that has spread throughout your entire body."

For over four hours, I sat in stunned silence as I listened to wave after wave of diagnoses. Midway through this session, Amanda stood up, and then walked outside to get some fresh air for herself.

"I just need a break," she said. "This is a lot to process."

Sensing our rising anxiety, the doctor looked at me and said, "Jim, I'm not your enemy or your friend. This is just science. Your blood doesn't lie."

As much as I hated hearing everything he shared, I listened and appreciated his straightforward approach. It wasn't his fault that I was in such bad shape. He was just telling me the truth.

Coming away from that conversation, I knew I needed to make some major changes. If I didn't, my physical health would face serious trouble. So, I chose life: I received that doctor's help. Following my doctor's advice, I cut out almost all carbs and sugar and took some natural supplements and hormone therapy to get my body back on track.

Six months after that wakeup call in Dr. Legome's office, we saw dramatic results! I had dropped nearly twenty pounds and started to feel strong and healthy. (Now, as of the final editing of this book in 2024, I've kept the weight off and I'm down 20 pounds!) I could certainly talk about the different habits I've put in place, such as physical exercise and less junk food, but the important point is that the real battle I face is in my mind, and I continue to pray for strength in this area.

For years I had thought a certain way about what it meant to live a healthy life. This way of thinking allowed me to eat generous portions of homemade chocolate chip cookies, Amanda's artisan sourdough bread (which is to die for!), macaroni and cheese, and pizza! That way of thinking was the problem. My health decline did not result from a one-time decision; instead, a series of micro-decisions, a thousand and one poor choices, and some genetic stuff out of my control coincided to take me on a frightening health trajectory. My doctor simply pointed out the destination if I did not change course. I could no longer snack multiple times a day with a muffin here or a bag of chips there. These eating habits worked their own forms of compound interest adding to my spare tire. These seemingly good decisions of "being a good Christian" by sacrificing physical activity times "to be with family" took a toll on my body that jeopardized my ability to be a healthy husband and father for my wife and kids.

Sure, deep down I always knew I had packed on extra weight, but I was really no different from other Americans in their late forties. Okay, I'll be blunt. I was fat. Truth is, many young kids and almost all middle aged and older Americans are overweight and unhealthy.

Not until that terrible morning in the doctor's office did I realize how compromised my health had become. I had developed unhealthy patterns, and I needed to think differently. I needed constant help every day. I needed to follow Dr. Amen's advice to retrain the neural pathways in my brain and form new healthy "ruts" or neural pathways. Although not an easy task, I found in myself the motivation to change. I knew what would happen if I didn't. Since that dark day in the doctor's office, every positive lifestyle choice I've made is the result of a series of battles I've fought and won *in my mind*.

Fighting those battles was made easier by being in a patient-doctor relationship with Dr. Meyers and Dr. Legome. They helped identify areas in my life that needed to change.

A Tribute to Dr. Legome

Dr. Martie Myers, wife of Dr. Mark Legome wanted to share some thoughts about her husband as Dr. Legome passed away January 3, 2023. He was 84 years old.

> "Dear God, thank you for your beautiful blessing. You gave me 26 years with Mark Legome. My husband, lover, partner, and best friend. He was a brilliant and compassionate man who truly cared and touched so many lives. Amen."
>
> *- Dr. Martie Myers*

The Mind

Spiritual victory begins in the mind. In *Battlefield of the Mind*, Joyce Meyer writes, "Satan knows well that if he can control our thoughts, he can control our actions."[29] She continues, "If our thoughts are going to affect what we become, then it should certainly be a priority that we think right thoughts."[30]

What we think shapes who we are and who we become—our character, identity, and ultimately our legacy. In the words of Craig Groeschel, "Our lives are always moving in the direction of our strongest thoughts."[31] There is an old saying that says you can't stop a bird from flying overhead, but you can prevent it from making a nest in your hair. Thoughts are much the same way. Some of the thoughts that enter our minds are beyond our control. But we can choose to allow the neural pathways in our

---

[29] Joyce Meyer, Battlefield of the Mind: Winning the Battle in Your Mind. FaithWords, 2008. Kindle edition. 16.
[30] Joyce Meyer, Battlefield of the Mind: Winning the Battle in Your Mind. FaithWords, 2008. Kindle edition. 19.
[31] Craig Groeschel, Winning the War in Your Mind: Change Your Thinking, Change Your Life

brains to form negative ruts, or we can train our minds to meditate on those things that are good.

In Philippians 4:8, the Apostle Paul writes, "Finally, brothers and sisters, whatever is true, whatever is noble, whatever is right, whatever is pure, whatever is lovely, whatever is admirable—if anything is excellent or praiseworthy—think about such things." Whenever we encounter a thought that falls outside the eight areas listed in this verse, we have a decision to make.

Let's say we encounter a thought like "You're stupid," "You'll never change," or "God would never forgive you." Now, what do we do with it? We can mumble to ourselves that we're an idiot and lend further support to this negative thought, or we can go back to the *truth* about our identity in Christ. We can remember that our identity is not determined by our temptations or by what we do. Our identity is found in Christ's victory over temptation (Hebrews 4:15) and by what Christ has accomplished on the cross (Colossians 2:13-15).

Philippians 4:8 is the model for the way we are to think. Every morning we wake up with a choice to move in the direction of strong, positive thoughts — or we can move toward things of little value. In *The 4:8 Principle*, Tommy Newberry writes, "The battle you wage against your human nature is an invisible one that will be won or lost in the mind. Minute by minute, hour by hour, in the hidden workshop of your mind, you are constructing thoughts of good or evil, depression or joy, success or failure."[32]

Thinking of the mind as a battlefield and choosing to reframe our thoughts and focus on a Philippians 4:8 mindset takes patience and determination. It's doing what 2 Corinthians 10:5 tells us to do: *taking ev-*

---

32 Tommy Newberry, *The 4:8 Principle*

ery thought captive. To solidify new ways of thinking, one of the practices Craig Groeschel recommends we follow is this helpful motto:

Write it.
Think it.
Confess it.
Until you believe it![33]

You can use this powerful, simple, four-step practice to retrain your brain. For example, let's say you're struggling with the habit of cussing. You know you shouldn't, but you find yourself slipping words into conversation that you know you shouldn't use. Rather than just making some ambiguous commitment to change, write out your resolve on a notecard or digital device. Write in your own words or copy a scripture verse like Philippians 4:8. This reminds me of Zig Ziglar's quote, "A goal properly set is halfway reached."

Commit that note to memory and confess that statement and verse to God throughout the day. Keep repeating this process until your internal belief results in positive outward action.

Retraining Sexuality

One of the ways I engaged in this battlefield of the mind occurred during my journey out of immoral sexuality. I had to retrain my brain to think in many new ways. I had bought into so many lies about my identity that each lie took a while to untangle.

I love what Romans 12:2 says when Paul urges his readers to "be transformed by the renewing of your mind." Paul's urgings healed my urges. His Spirit-inspired words resonated in my mind day after day and kept

---

[33] https://www.instagram.com/p/CMKJ41ZJ-J8/?hl=en

me focused on the work of God in my life. I was on a journey where God graciously renewed the way I thought about reality.

At the time, I had developed a whole host of destructive habits – symptoms of the way I thought. Aside from sex with multiple partners, I drank too much and had a filthy mouth. I'll never forget when, during the years in my sinful past, I was on the phone with a customer service representative. Every other word out of my mouth was a cuss word. Within a few minutes, I heard her voice crack on the other end of the line, and she said as politely as she could, "Sir, I'll have to disconnect you from this call because the words you're saying are hurting me." Her words pierced my heart like a dagger; I felt terrible, like the curtain of my sinful heart was pulled back for a couple seconds and revealed the horrible person I had become.

When I came back to Christ, I knew these sinful habits had to change. The only way I could do this was by focusing on passages like Romans 12 and allowing God to renew and transform my mind. It's a constant fact: the battle of the mind remains the hardest fight I have. That's why I need "constant help."

If you are just starting out on this journey, my encouragement to you would be to start with the big stuff. Are you practicing habits today which cause harm to your physical body? If so, tackle those first. Next, work on your habits that cause harm or destruction to others.

When I first started my commitment to break free of my list of sinful habits, someone confronted me about using chewing tobacco (my alternative vice to puffing on cigarettes). He had a point, but I snapped at him with my response. "Look, man," I began, "I'm trying to focus on not having sex outside of marriage!"

Today I understand that taking up a new sin to help stop a different sin is not strategic or logical. The truth is simply this: Some days I mess up. I allow thoughts that want to distort my sense of identity in Christ.

Thinking back to that time when I was so defensive and barking out, "Look, man!" gives me empathy today for those who are still struggling to break free of harmful addictions that feel too overwhelming to defeat. This journey of breaking sin's grasp is not for the faint of heart: it is tough! But what makes it tougher than it should be is when we try in our strength to win the battle by ourselves without getting help.

Get help. Start with the big things first, and let God continue to work on the ways you think and behave in the smaller areas of your life. Don't forget to ride with others who can help you. Some of the best help that you can ever get is from your wife and from other women who have expertise. Listen to your physician and spend time with other men who will be honest with you. You have a body, and you're in charge of keeping in shape. You have a mind, and it's your job to renew it in God's Word.

The Science of the Brain

This whole idea of retraining our brains and renewing our minds is anchored in Scripture; but it is also rooted in science, in what we call the field of neuroscience. Christian psychiatrist, Curt Thompson, summarizes it this way:

"As you may know, your brain is made up of a left and a right hemisphere. While both sides of the brain are involved in just about every activity, the two hemispheres function differently. The left hemisphere processes in a logical and sequential manner; the right hemisphere processes in a more intuitive and holistic way. The two hemispheres function best when they are integrated. In fact, neuroscience confirms much of what Scripture teaches us about the importance of living with undivided hearts and minds. While it is true that we each have separate brains, our minds are interconnected in many complex and mysterious ways."[34]

---

[34] Anatomy of the Soul: Surprising Connections between Neuroscience and Spiritual Practices That Can Transform Your Life and Relationships. Tyndale House Publishers,

RETRAIN YOUR BRAIN

This interconnectivity is important. Often, we might hear someone speak of having a more right-brain versus a left-brain way of thinking. But as Thompson notes, the goal is to bring both together. "I believe our lives will be abundant, joyful, and peaceful only to the degree that we are engaged, known, and understood by one another." He continues with this observation, "I also believe we cannot separate what we do with our brains and our relationships from what we do with God. God has designed our minds, part of his good creation, to invite us into a deeper, more secure, more courageous relationship with him and with one another."[35]

In other words, we allow the truth of God's Word to reshape the neural pathways in our minds so that we can think as God would want us to think. We bring not just one side of our minds under his control, but the totality of our right and left brains. And as we bring these two together, we start to think differently about our lives and God's creation.

As Tommy Newberry points out, "The secret conversations you hold in the privacy of your own mind are shaping your destiny, little by little."[36] While there are some addictions that can bring utter devastation to our brains and make it difficult for us to be restored to our prior states, most addictions we have can be corrected through learning to think the right way. *In a literal sense, when we put on our new selves, we are creating new neural pathways in our brains.* We are teaching ourselves new ways to think, and thus behave.

In a literal sense, when we put on our new selves, we are creating new neural pathways in our brains. We are teaching ourselves new ways to think, and thus behave.

Inc.. Kindle Edition. Location 226.
35 Anatomy of the Soul: Surprising Connections between Neuroscience and Spiritual Practices That Can Transform Your Life and Relationships. Tyndale House Publishers, Inc.. Kindle Edition. Location 226.
36 Tommy Newberry, *The 4:8 Principle*

Just Say No

Going back to that conversation I had in my doctor's office, one of the major hurdles I had to overcome was my love of sugar. I've been attached to some addictive stuff, but sugar is arguably the most addictive element on the planet! Try to find any food product in America that does not contain sugar. Most manufactured foods contain some type or form of sugar (including genetically modified) to addict people to their products.

Sugar is bad for you. I've read the research on how sugar can contribute to cancer and be detrimental to one's health. But I still love it. "C&H Pure Cane Sugar, that's the one." If you're old enough to remember this little jingle, join the old man club! It still rings in my ear to this day. White sugar, brown sugar, corn syrup — you name it – our foods are laced with sugar. Buy a package of bacon and it, too, is loaded with sugar!

So, I love sugar, and I also love bread. But here is the problem: if your body does not burn the carbohydrates in all the bread you eat, guess what happens? Yup, it all converts to sugar. When this sugar is not burned, it is converted to fat. Thus, it comes as no surprise that America is one of the fattest nations on the planet.

Flashback to when Dr. Legome gave me the initial news about my bloodwork. The good news was that most of it could be fixed through diet and exercise. In May 2022, I cut out grain carbs, sugar, and processed foods. To better make my course correction, I even temporarily cut out raw fruits and vegetables that contained natural sugars.

This dramatic change allowed me to drop ten pounds in the first few months. My new diet lifestyle was inspired by the Paleo diet which focuses on eating meats, fruits, and vegetables. After making this switch—and cutting out yeast—I noticed my body took a turn in the right direction. Yeast is a beast, at least for me. So, I stopped eating bread products, and that helped me a lot.

I'll be honest again: This new lifestyle has been far from easy. Days 2 and 3 were especially difficult. It's only as I have intentionally cut sugar out of my diet that I've realized how prevalent sugar is in our society. I'm amazed at the amount of sugar offered to my children from places of business, church, school, friends, neighbors, and family. It's relentless. But I keep making the choice to say "no." That's part of what it means to "choose life."

Thinking a New Way

Soon after returning to Christ, a pastor asked me to share my story in front of a congregation of 1,000 people.

After I finished, a young man named Rhett approached me at the outdoor welcome center of our church. The epitome of "tall, dark, and handsome," he was from Florida, and he came across to me as an all-American type of dude. Rhett grew up in Georgia and was an avid soccer player.

"Ah…Jim, I have a favor to ask. Can you forgive me? I do not know what to do. I'm asking for your forgiveness because of the way I have treated gay men. I've made fun of them, teased them, and said unkind things about them. God has convicted me of my heart towards them and wanted me to speak with you."

I forgave Rhett on the spot and thanked him for his sensitivity to the Lord's prompting. Little did I know that this would be the start of a strong relationship. Rhett and I would become good friends and still are today. A few years after my marriage to Amanda, Rhett followed my lead, and married the girl of his dreams. Although he dealt with different sin issues than I faced, I've been able to walk with him and help him have greater freedom in his walk with Jesus. Here's a piece of his story:

Rhett had not kept his virginity and was sexually active with multiple women prior to marriage. He asked me if I could help him now that he had committed his life to Christ. He was desiring to make Jesus Lord of his life, and this included his sexual behaviors. As a man in his twenties, he had stopped having sex with other women but had shifted his attention to pornography. Rhett was not a porn addict, but he had a habit of replacing sex outside of marriage with another destructive behavior. He tried to satisfy his legitimate sexual desires with unhealthy and destructive patterns.

After taking Rhett through Neil Anderson's *Steps to Freedom in Christ*, Rhett confessed his past relationships, dealt with his porn addiction, and was set free. Today, in his 30s, Rhett has remained faithful to his wife, and today they have four children. For years, Rhett developed a pattern of thinking that led him to act out in unhealthy ways. He wrongly assumed that a little bit of pornography was a safe alternative to having sex with women outside of marriage. Mistakenly, he thought that holding all these thoughts to himself was the best way to cope with his problems. But when he tried to handle things all by himself, he lost the battle.

Rhett broke through this wall by getting help. By being honest. And when he received help in friendship with me and others, things changed. When Rhett focused on dealing with core issues holding him back, and then retrained his brain to think in the right way, he experienced genuine freedom. He, too, broke away from sin's grasp.

> **Helpful Hint:** Have you considered that when you watch pornography, you are supporting human and child trafficking? Remember, all men and women are created in the image of God, and we all bear His image. The money made through the pornography industry fuels human trafficking. What if that was your daughter? Your son? Your brother or sister, or sibling in Christ whom you were viewing? Reflecting on this thought can give you a new motivation to stop.

Steps to Freedom

Retraining our brains takes time. Going back to my "come to Jesus" moment in the doctor's office, the retraining of my brain resulted in positive outward action. In addition to the other pleasures, I gave up, I said good-bye to beer and wine and will occasionally enjoy whiskey or even better vodka – tripled distilled. Do you need to give up certain alcohols? Or avoid them altogether? I eat more meat, proteins, and vegetables. I split meals with my wife when we go out to eat, thus lowering my calorie intake and saving a few extra bucks. I don't consume dairy anymore; I use almond or oat milk. Instead of going to a Mexican restaurant and picking any item on the menu, I order steak fajitas and get an extra serving of meat or veggies. I forego the chips and make sure to place them beyond arm's length, and I have extra hot salsa as my reward.

As I see it, my health journey is living proof that anyone can make a change. If I can do it, given my past track record of huge failure, others can do it too with the help of God. Of course, we cannot attain perfection, but we can always find ways to improve. If you have a sin habit in your life that needs to change, I will offer several suggestions.

First, identify your major issue. What needs to change? Write down your resolve and commit to some clear steps of action. Make a stated declaration that things *will* be different.

Second, find a replacement. What can you do to replace your poor habit(s)? If you need help with this, consider the healthy activities you enjoy. What's your favorite hobby or pastime? How do you treat yourself? Is it fishing, hunting, playing a sport, or going to the movies? Reach out to a trusted friend or counselor to better develop these coaching techniques. Decide what you must do to succeed.

Third, plan for temptation and think strategically. For example, before I travel out of state to a speaking event, I'll reach out to my male accountability partners and ask them to keep me accountable. The mind war can begin before, during, or after an event. As my spiritual walk has matured, I've noticed the enemy predictably attacks after large, significant events. The pressure of preparing for the talk is over, and my mind can often take me to places I shouldn't go. This normally happens after the "big high" and success of an event and the natural letdown after the pomp and circumstance. By alerting my accountability partners and checking in with them, I'm able to avoid failure and remain on the path to spiritual victory. It's funny, but sometimes we develop a misconception of what strong self-control should look like. As James Clear notes,

"The people with the best self-control are typically the ones who need to use it the least. It's easier to practice self-restraint when you don't have to use it very often. So, yes, perseverance, grit, and willpower are essential to success, but the way to improve these qualities is not by wishing you were a more disciplined person, but by creating a more disciplined environment."[37]

Fourth, confess and repent if you fail. While you should never intend to fall, the potential for failure always looms as a clear reality if we remain on our spiritual journey for any length of time. However, the key to freedom involves responding to failure the right way. We don't excuse or justify our sins. Instead, we confess our faults to God and others and move forward.

Application

1. Who are you inviting to join you on your journey of retraining your brain? Ask them now! You could ask something like this: what areas of victory have you had using the concepts from the chapter?

---

37 James Clear, Atomic Habits: An Easy & Proven Way to Build Good Habits & Break Bad Ones. Penguin Publishing Group, 2018. Kindle edition. 93.

2. **Action Item:** For each issue you want to change, compare it to the eight qualities in Philippians 4:8. Meditate on the godly quality that is most relevant to your area of battle.

CHAPTER 7

RISE ABOVE

You, dear children, are from God and have overcome them, because the one who is in you is greater than the one who is in the world.

1 John 4:4

Sometimes the weight of rising above our challenges feels overwhelming. During my childhood, I attended Rose Drive Friends Church with Trent Douglass—who was five years older than I. Trent grew up in a Christian home with parents who went to church. Life was good. But when he was thirteen, his father committed adultery, and everything changed for Trent. Prior to this, Trent assumed his dad was a great Christian and father. This new revelation sent him into a tailspin.

Angry at his father's decisions, Trent gave up on church and jumped into a life of sin. It wasn't long before he found himself doing all sorts of things he'd never imagined doing.

Pornography caught his attention. He started doing hard drugs like crystal meth, cocaine, and LSD to ease his troubled mind. Ever the entrepreneur, Trent decided to maximize his personal drug addiction by turning it into a source of personal gain. After building a treehouse-style platform in one of his backyard trees, Trent started his own marijuana farm above the eyesight of family members and neighbors.

Trent's mini empire started to grow, and before long Trent developed a reputation as *the* drug dealer of Yorba Linda. His life didn't look that bad, so long as he didn't get caught. But when he turned fifteen, Trent's reckless lifestyle started to catch up with him, and he was arrested multiple times. He ended up with a serious charge for felony arson that began one day when Trent and his buddies were bored. They decided to ride down to the local convenience store and smuggle bottles of vodka under their coats — an act they had committed and gotten away with numerous times before. After yet another successful heist, the boys headed home. On their way, they passed a series of apartment buildings with a row of cars parked out front. By this point, they were more than a little drunk, and that's when Trent made a treacherous decision that he would later regret.

Seeing a can of gasoline sitting beside one of the cars, he promptly snatched the container, emptied the contents onto the rear of one of the vehicles, and struck a match. Within seconds, the car was engulfed in flames. For obvious reasons, Trent and his buddies made a speedy exit.

To Trent's dismay, local law enforcement officers quickly pieced together what had happened. Merely minutes later, Trent was apprehended, his hands still reeking of gasoline. After a failed attempt to convince the officers that he had been working on his lawnmower, the cops asked Trent for his mom's contact info. At the time, she was working at the local juvenile detention home, causing one of the cops to sarcastically remark, "Well, that's good because you'll be seeing her soon!"

In the 80s, if you wanted a poster child for a young man with a messed up life, Trent was your guy. His run-ins with the law continued. Still fifteen, Trent sideswiped two vehicles while driving his buddy's car. Not wanting to face the consequences of his actions, Trent left his friend's car and ran home. As it turned out, his mom was just about to leave town to visit her mom, and Trent begged her to take him along. Just as they were about to head out the door, the phone rang.

"Don't answer it, Mom," Trent begged.

But it was too late. Apparently, word around town had identified Trent as the guilty culprit, and a friend of the family called to say that the cops were out looking for him.

Busted once again.

For the next few years, Trent tried everything to be happy. He moved in with his girlfriend, continued selling drugs, enjoyed more than his share of alcohol, and stayed addicted to pornography. As Trent shares, it wasn't as if he didn't know any better. He did. In fact, he felt constant conviction. He knew his actions were wrong and felt miserable about his choices. Yet, in the back of his mind, he feared that if he became a Christian, he'd stop having fun and ruin his life.

The Power of Confession

Trent's problem wasn't that he didn't know right from wrong. It wasn't that he didn't want to rise above his challenges. His real problem was that he didn't want to change. He feared that if he went God's way and confessed his sins, he wouldn't have any fun; instead, he'd be confined to a life of boredom. Years later, Trent would look back on this time and admit, "Little did I know I'd have way more fun being a Christian!"

Sadly, the story of Trent's upbringing is not that uncommon. Sure, not everyone becomes the drug dealer of their city, but many of us know the pain of disappointment and loss. Maybe a family member or friend broke a promise or didn't hold up their end of the relationship. These kinds of situations leave us reeling, feeling unsure of how to respond. But rather than running toward God, we run away from Him. That was my story, too, for quite a few years.

Like Trent and me, everyone has his own story of personal rebellion against God. The question is not whether we have sinned, but what we will do with our sinful pasts. Will we ignore our sins or think our sins are too great for God to handle?

I John 1:9 tells us, if we confess our sins to God, he is faithful and just to forgive us of our sins. And not only that, his blood cleanses us from all unrighteousness. Verbal confession is powerful, because it is a declaration to God and others of what you know to be true. Confession liberates. It releases the chains the enemy seeks to use to hold us back.

The idea of *repentance* comes on the heels of *confession*. When we confess with our mouth that "Jesus is Lord," and we repent of our sinful past, we essentially make a grand course correction. We do a U-turn. We move away from the man we used to be and move toward God. As we take this step, something wonderful happens: our title switches from "Sinner" to "Saint." This doesn't mean we turn into super Christians who suddenly become incapable of sin, but it does mean our primary identity is no longer defined by our old nature.

Whenever the Apostle Paul wrote a letter to a church, it's worth noting how he addressed himself: he called himself *a servant of God* or *a servant of Christ*. Romans 1:1, "Paul, a servant of Christ Jesus, called to be an apostle and set apart for the gospel of God." He recognized his primary identity and his new nature with Christ and discarded his past identity and nature. Nowhere in Scriptures are we called to be "saved sinners." Instead, we are called to be *saints*. We are children of God, created for a purpose and a plan, as Paul encourages us in Ephesians 2:10:

"For we are God's handiwork, created in Christ Jesus to do good works, which God prepared in advance for us to do."

> *"For we are God's handiwork, created in Christ Jesus to do good works, which God prepared in advance for us to do."*

Something that drives me crazy about Christendom is our acceptance of sin. *We can't do better than this*, we tell ourselves. We focus on the depravity rather than on the righteousness of the renewed spirit. Unfortunately, so many Christian authors and writers deal with *sin management* rather than *sin eradication*. I'm not trying to preach "holier than thou," but instead point our attention to the freedom Jesus offers. Yes, I still mess up and have not arrived. I'm in this with you! That's why I'm in need of the Savior, Jesus! Speaking about what Jesus has accomplished for us, James Bryan Smith writes:

> "He cleansed us and regenerated us, and he is now living in and through us. This was accomplished, it was completed…It happened in and through the work of the Trinity, long before you and I were born. Jesus died for my sins before I committed even one. Jesus rose from the grave to offer me new life before I knew I needed it. He did it all; I did nothing to merit this. But upon my confession of faith and new birth, Christ is now my life (Colossians 3:4). I no longer live, but Christ lives in me (Galatians 2:20)."[38]

When it comes to our approach to Christ, we can take two damaging routes. Both stem from an inflated view of self. The first says, *"I'm too good for God; I am fine without Him."* This is pride. But the second says, *"I'm too bad for God; he would never come to someone like me."* This too is a form of pride because it inflates the power of self and puts limits on the reach of God. We dare to tell God that we know better than He does. When we speak lies, we try to turn God into a liar (I John 1:10).

But when we decide to be truthful enough to confess our sins, God's power begins to change us.

---

38 James Bryan Smith, *The Good and Beautiful You*, 146

The Power of Divine Transformation

After turning 17, Trent moved in with his girlfriend and her father. Eventually her dad kicked them both out of the house, and Trent moved in with his mom, who continued to pray for Trent with every wrong turn he took. She'd preach the gospel to him and pray with Trent's friend's mom every Thursday night.

For a few more years, Trent hopped around between relationships, high on drugs and addicted to porn. It wasn't until he turned 21 that things began to change. It started when his younger brother Rob's fiancée broke off their engagement, which brought Trent's brother to his knees and challenged him to get right with God. Rob was radically saved! At the beginning of Trent's brother's transformation, Rob began to date a new girl (who would later become his wife) and started witnessing to her. She was a "backslidden" Christian, but he began reading Scripture to her on their first date. Thanks to Rob's influence, she quickly recommitted her life to Christ. Believe it or not, they've been missionaries and pastors ever since.

Trent's brother, Rob, even started a Bible study in their mom's backyard. (Notice that God answered their mom's prayers!) Thankfully, their mom, Deanna, remarried a loving and godly man. God was providing healing for their whole family.

One night after the Bible study in the backyard, Trent came in through the back door of the house and went straight into his bedroom. Falling to his knees, he cried out to God and asked to be set free. In the back of his mind, Trent knew that on his own, he could not break free of habits like drugs and alcohol. Trent realized his addiction to porn was unbreakable by his own strength.

This prompted Trent to make a deal with God: "God, if you can save me, then I'm willing. But I don't think I'm savable," he grieved. "I think I'm so bound in my sin."

Unwilling to make a full commitment, Trent struck what he thought was a reasonable deal with God and decided, by negotiation, to give God one full week of his life. As Trent often jokes today, that week started on August 15, 1991, and has continued to this day, making it the longest week ever recorded in human history!

Through God's power, Trent found the strength to rise above the destructive habits of his past. He started to engage in his younger brother's Thursday night Bible study which grew into a thriving community. Friends of Trent, who had seen him at his lowest, started to show up, and their small group of curious friends grew to over 200 people.

During these gatherings, they would have "burn parties" where attendees threw their porn magazines or other sinful material into the fire. Trent and his group did anything they could to reach others. They'd hand out business card invitations with a BYOB (Bring Your Own Bible) request attached — prompting some invitees to misinterpret this and bring a six-pack of beer instead of a Bible! Given that this all took place during the height of the LA riots, law enforcement would sometimes show up at these gatherings expecting a wild party. Instead, they found a group of people worshipping Jesus.

Despite the transformed lives, the city issued an ultimatum that Trent's group would need to move its location. Soon after the move, this Bible study became a church with Trent as the lead pastor—a miracle in and of itself! Being dyslexic and barely able to read the menu at a restaurant, Trent felt certain there was no way he could become a preacher of God's Word. He believed that so many others were much more qualified, though it soon became evident to Trent and others that he had a spiritual gift God wanted him to use.

In 1995, Trent and his team launched Calvary Chapel Saving Grace, the same church he pastors to this present day. Every week, Trent shares with the congregation that they too can rise above any challenges they have faced. It doesn't matter if someone is a drug or porn addict, God can change a life and empower anyone to become a major force for good in this world.

Today, in addition to being a pastor, Trent runs a large international ministry called Saving Grace World Missions. His church has been instrumental in planting over one-hundred churches around the globe. Trent's primary focus is to help unbelievers located in the 10/40 window (Northern Africa, the Middle East, and South Asia) to know the saving power of Jesus Christ. He strongly supports Christian Bible Schools and makes frequent trips overseas to encourage and support pastors in any way he can.

This is the power of divine transformation.

A Mom's Encouragement: Deanna (Douglass) Fletcher's Intercession for Her Two Sons

You can count on Satan to interfere when God's plans are huge. Recognize this and realize who your real enemy is. It is not your spouse nor your kids. There is a roaring lion looking for those that God plans to use.

It is time to get your armor on (Ephesians 6:10-18). Your fight is not with those you love, but with that roaring lion. Satan's plans are to interfere with God's mighty works.

Our husbands are being challenged and bombarded daily with this ungodly world. You can keep his clothes washed, his stomach full, and the house nice, but it's going to take a lot more than these things. Satan is looking to destroy families.

I once lost that battle, but I refuse to allow Satan to have his way again. The ripple effect of sin and divorce spreads wide. Our children, also, are being bombarded with sin more than any time in history. Children without the covering of a dad in the home hurt more than we realize. They soon start hunting for love and acceptance in all the wrong places. Beware!

You must dress purposely, with the complete armor of God. There were times that I had to sleep with it on. You must keep in the Word and believe God's promises.

Find a Godly mom who is also struggling with her children. Meet at least once a week for intense prayer. Fight on your knees and stay focused. Pray together for one child at a time, until you have exhausted all matters. Then move on to the next child. Pray away wrong friends. Pray for their teachers and all those who speak into their lives. Pray God will replace all bad influences with Godly ones. Pray that God will get the glory.

JUST DON'T GIVE UP!

Receive your advice from only God's Word and keep standing on His promises. Seek out a caring pastor to meet with as often as possible. I saw two of my pastors at least once a week. I thank God for their counsel.

Stay strong—physically, mentally, and spiritually. I also was being attacked from all areas. The lion and the wolves were chasing me down. I had many sleepless nights.

My pastor, Chuck Mylander, gave me the challenge to write my prayers down in a journal, keeping it next to my bed. Write my prayers down each night and then shut the book, let God handle the situation, and go to sleep thanking Him for what He's going to do. It worked. I got the rest I needed.

Stay bold! I have ripped posters off of my son's bedroom walls, poured stuff down the toilet in front of them. Once I even flagged down a police car and went to his window before he could get out. I explained that I had to go to work and could not get my junior higher to get out of bed for school. I gave the officer my address, told him my door was unlocked and asked him to go and wake him up. He said yes. (Sorry I missed that scene.)

Our children are on loan to us, and we need to recognize that they belong to the Lord. Only Jesus Christ can calm all the ripples in the storms. We are to stand firm, believing His promises, and keep fighting on our knees. He will keep His word and give us the peace we so desperately need and desire. But watch out! Your prayers may be answered in way bigger ways than you can ever imagine (Eph.3:20). In the midst of the storm, I kept reminding myself, "IT'S NOT THE END OF THE STORY"!

- Mom of Trent and Rob, Deanna Fletcher

Do Your Part

Rising above sinful habits happens as we do our part and trust God to do his. God's part includes dying for our sins, offering us forgiveness, and empowering us to live above sin. Our part is to take God at his word and walk in all the light we have been given. And as we walk in harmony with the Holy Spirit, his strength empowers us to be who God would want us to be.

Neil Anderson writes: "Even though Satan is defeated, he still rules this world through a hierarchy of demons who tempt, accuse, and deceive those who fail to put on the armor of God, stand firm in their faith, and take every thought captive to the obedience of Christ. Our sanctuary is our identity and position in Christ, and we have all the protection we need to live a victorious life, but if we fail to assume our responsibility and give ground to Satan, we will suffer the consequences of our sinful attitudes and actions. The good news is, we can repent and reclaim all that we have in Christ, and that is what *The Steps* will enable you to do."[39]

The closer we get to God, the more we want to become like him. This realization should motivate us to get rid of anything in our lives that inhibits our walk with Christ. There are many ways to do this, and sometimes extreme measures are called for—based on how severe the addictions or

---

[39] Anderson, Neil T. *The Steps to Freedom in Christ: A Biblical Guide to Help You Resolve Personal and Spiritual Conflicts and Become a Fruitful Disciple of Jesus*. Baker Publishing Group, 2017. Kindle edition. 7.

strongholds are that have held you captive. Even Jesus spoke of such examples in Matthew 18:8-9 when he warned, "If your hand or foot causes you to sin, cut it off and cast it from you." In the spirit of Jesus' warning, here are a few things to consider.

- **Change** the stuff you listen to and watch. Which tunes or movies remind you of the life you used to live? Distance yourself from this material.
- **Remove** social media apps on your phone that distract you.
- **Get rid** of all material possessions connected to the sinful lifestyle you were living. If you've had sex outside of marriage in your bed, get rid of your old bed.
- **Move!** Move to a new location so you aren't passing those same places that brought you down; or move away from people in your past.
- **Delete** photos that no longer represent the life you have in Christ.
- **Change** your phone number and get a new mobile device if necessary.

I could continue, but you get the point. *The idea is to eliminate strongholds and items that contain memories, conscious and unconscious, of sinful things you've done.* What are those items for you? Ask the Holy Spirit to guide and direct you, and he will reveal what items you need to eliminate. He won't necessarily give you a checklist. For me, the process spanned a handful of years. Whenever I'd ask him, he would gently remind me to get rid of an item. I even got rid of one of my favorite Bibles that I had with me during my sinful sexual life.

A key turning point in my life happened in the summer of 2002. I had a younger cousin who was set free from demonic possession. When she entered a relationship with Jesus, she wanted as much of Him as she could get, so she eliminated anything that got in the way of this pursuit. In fact, I remember her asking me while I was sexually immoral, "Jim, if you know the truth, how can you keep living as a gay man?" She couldn't understand my choice to keep sinning, as she truly knew the unseen powerful forces of darkness in the heavenly realms as a demon occupied her body until it was exorcized from her, and she gave her life to Jesus.

When I finally came back to Christ, I chose to take my cousin to the Huntington Beach fire pits and got rid of everything that connected me to my sinful past. After I got the fire going, I threw everything into it: inappropriate underwear, leather chaps, and all other items connected to my previous life. The fire began to rage higher and higher, illuminating the dark sky to a red-amber glow, while sparks and embers snapped, crackled, and popped into the cool ocean breeze.

My cousin understood. She herself had given her life to Jesus after having a demon exorcised from her. I wasn't demon-possessed in my former life, but during those years, I did choose death. Now I was choosing life, and my cousin was there to help me.

To be clear, the whole idea behind taking these drastic steps is not to embrace some form of works-based salvation. Rather, I was aiming to do everything I could to forge a straight path in my walk with God.

In culture, we often admire people, like former Navy Seal David Goggins, who preaches a relentless style of self-discipline. But when it comes to discipline in our spiritual lives, we sometimes despise those who take seriously the need for discipline. It is true that Satan uses legalism to destroy the faith of many, but when we act like any restrictions are vestiges of "legalism" that infringe upon our rights, we aren't being honest enough to choose life.

Do your part. Decide who you want to go with you to rid your house of junk that you don't need. For me, it was my cousin because she understood. Who is it for you?

A Father We Can Trust

Looking back, Trent can see that many of his challenges in life came from a warped understanding of fatherhood. When his dad walked out on him, he felt as though he had lost his sense of identity. The "rock" he thought he could depend on had betrayed him. Such a painful loss prompted Trent to search for love in all the wrong places. Because he did not grow up with a father as a role model, Trent spent much of his childhood feeling abandoned and hurt. He still remembers the time his dad promised to get back together with his mom, only to reach out a few days later to say he was gone for good.

Only as Trent began to understand that God is his heavenly Father, a faithful Father who will not let him down, did he experience healing. He recognized that the hole in his life could only be filled by God. The desire for his heavenly Father soon replaced the longings he felt to know his earthly father. As Trent often points out, many Christians are so quick to focus on Jesus that they overlook the Fatherhood of God.

In a fatherless society, having a proper understanding of God as Father is critical to the integrity of our spiritual journey. In fact, everything Jesus did pointed to the Father. Jesus was here on Earth to "be about his Father's business." Today, Trent is a father of four, with his oldest son serving as youth pastor. While Trent has undoubtedly messed up at various times, he makes it clear to his kids that their true Father is God.

In a fatherless society, having a proper understanding of God as Father is critical to the integrity of our spiritual journey.

As Trent points out, Jesus has come to this earth to reveal his Father to the world. Trent can trust *this* Father. So can you and I. When we understand God as our Father, we understand that He is big enough and strong enough for any problems we face. When we get trapped in sin, we don't hide *from* the Father, we run *to* the Father. Trent's strong belief in God as a Father empowers him to go to the darkest regions of the world to proclaim the gospel. This conviction compels him to do work in the Muslim and Hindu world instead of enjoying the comforts of his cozy office in luxurious Orange County, California.

As I wrote in my first book, *Not a Mistake*, I wrestled with my own share of "daddy wounds." No, my dad didn't walk out on my family, and he was in many respects a great dad. But still, I was wounded in deep ways. It was only in my thirties that I established a real relationship with my dad. I make this point because, if you're reading this book, there is a good chance you have your own father wounds that might contribute to a poor understanding of Father God.

If this is the case, I want to offer you some encouragement: God loves you. He cares for you. He is there for you. He will never leave or forsake you. He is near to the brokenhearted and close to those who are in pain. So, seek him, long for him, and desire him with your whole heart. Together, with his strength pumping through your veins, you will be empowered to rise above any habits of sin you face.

Three Paths

As I bring this book to a close, I'm reminded of a blast from my childhood. Do you remember those *Choose Your Own Adventure* books? These stories allow readers to be the star of the narrative and make such decisions as entering a dark forest or climbing a mountain. Each decision takes you down a different path. *Choose Your Own Adventure* books are a lot like life! We encounter countless forks in the road that present us with numerous options. Sometimes these are choices between life and death, though most of the time they appear to be small decisions that result in similar outcomes. It is here—in the small decisions—that we need the Holy Spirit to guide us and assist us in our decision-making.

After counseling hundreds of men to Break Sin's Grasp, they have risen above patterns of habitual sin. I've realized everyone's "journey to breakthrough" is different. Yes, core principles like confession, repentance, and accountability still apply to all. But because each person is wired differently, this means that what works for one personality might not work for another. We all have different learning styles.

Every person's path forward is contingent on where they are when they begin. For example, if you have struggled with a habit or major addiction for many years, you're going to require some intense counseling and a structured process to help you form new patterns of behavior. If you're someone who struggles with occasionally looking at pornography, you need a software program, like Covenant Eyes, and a strong accountability partner to help you change.

To help clarify which path you might be on, I have created three areas that might help you discern your next steps for coaching.

Path 1: Uncontrollable Addiction

Addicts rarely think of themselves as addicts, but maybe you struggle with one or more of these areas and you can't stop:

- Viewing pornography
- Acting out sexually outside of a marriage relationship
- Masturbation
- Drugs, marijuana, tobacco, and/or alcohol
- Food abuse and overeating

If there is an area of your life where you wish you could stop, but can't, you have become enslaved to an addiction and you need help.

Path 2: Unhealthy Behavior

Unhealthy behavior is not limited to the issues mentioned above; it also includes how they are played out. I vividly remember meeting with two men who were former homosexuals, because I wanted to find men who had left the lifestyle and lived a "normal" life. One was a college professor, married, and had a couple of kids. The other man was single, but both seemed to be healthy, functioning adults.

These two men shared their stories with me, and I shared mine. Then one of them asked me a pointed question: "Do you have any addictions?"

"No," I emphatically responded.

"OK, how often do you look at porn?"

I paused for a moment and said, "Ugh…once a month maybe. But I can stop whenever I want to. I just choose to look at it occasionally."

That's when the guy had the audacity to look at me and say, "If you're looking at porn once a month, then stop. Prove you're not addicted."

At first, I felt rather insulted, but I took his comment to heart and decided to stop looking at porn to prove I was not an addict.

I'm sharing this conversation because it was a reality check for me. These men caught me dead in my tracks of sin and my repeated unhealthy behavior. When I was confronted by them, I could see the chains on me that I had not seen before. Part of the "constant help" I need is loving confrontation that opens my eyes to what I can't see on my own.

Now I can truthfully say that I am "not addicted" to porn.

Path 3: Needs Fine Tuning

Maybe you're not addicted to a sin and have cut out most unhealthy behaviors in your life, but there are still smaller areas of life in need of change.

For me, I point back to Chapter 6 and the story of when my doctor confronted me about my eating habits. Prior to that point, I thought I was on the right track. Only after I was confronted with the scientific results of my bloodwork, did I realize that I had subtly drifted "off mission." Suddenly, the narrative that I had told myself was manifestly busted. I knew it was not true on account of the new information I had received. Knowledge is light. Only in the light could I finally come to realize that, for me, the gig was up: I needed to change. Because I honestly, in my heart, wanted to experience the greater freedom that a healthier style of eating good food brings, I made the decision to change.

How did I do it? By walking in the Light. I John 1:7 says, "If we walk in the Light as He Himself is in the Light, we have fellowship with one another, and the blood of Jesus His Son cleanses us from all sin."

Imagine each of these three pathways merging on the road toward freedom. If you're coming off addiction, you will need to merge onto the road earlier than someone who is overcoming unhealthy behaviors. Similarly, if you're a Christian who is looking to fine-tune your walk, your pathway will begin further down the road. But wherever you merge, we are all in this together, walking together towards greater freedom in Christ.

A Call to Rise

Everyone has flaws. We all make mistakes. Everyone is beset with a sinful nature. These are facts and are to be expected. But one of the greatest sins we can ever commit is the sin of omission. Rather than seek to experience greater freedom, we can choose to cower to the moment and remain bound in chains that hold us back.

Today's culture is sex-confused, which stems from the philosophical narrative that says you can change your biological sex. This confusion – propagated by the LGBTQ agenda on social media logarithms, television, government, and public education in the United States — has created a social-engineering experiment with catastrophic results. This confusion distorts reality, and the hyper-sexualization of children creates sinful issues and traps from which people cannot break free. I am witnessing a host of sexual issues for young people who desire freedom at levels I've never seen.

But instead of choosing to rise to the challenge, many men are conquered by their weakness. Men are pressured by culture to stay silent, isolate themselves and hide in a so-called "man cave."

This inclination to nurture an "I don't want to rock the boat" mentality keeps men in bondage. As men who are trying to be calm and in control, we don't want to offend anyone or come across as failures. That's why we decide to do nothing. But this sin of inaction and so-called "manly" silence spawns the advance of evil. The enemy roars like a lion, and we let him ravish our communities and families—and our own souls.

This call to rise is for men to fight and be bold! Rather than shrivel, be courageous. Tackle evil! Battle temptations! Take every thought captive to Christ!

And don't try to do it all alone.

Urging Men to Choose Life!

I see this time in history as a great opportunity for revival to happen among men in local churches. "In my study of the revivals of history," Daniel Henderson writes, "I am convinced that people were not seeking 'revival.' Most of what I have observed about revival was the result of common people seeking God for an uncommon work of the indwelling Holy Spirit."[40] I believe revival is about Christians who know God and

---

40 Henderson, Daniel. Transforming Presence: How the Holy Spirit Changes Everything-From the Inside Out (pp. 203-204). Moody Publishers. Kindle Edition.

choose to walk in freedom. As we Christians share our stories with each other and others, we can together seek God's face. To usher in a spiritual awakening in America and in other countries, we need men who respect their "constant need" for help. During my mission statement session with Dr. Sarah Sumner, I told her I love men "because men get things done." If you want to see something done, something big, like the establishment of a new city, or the building of a high rise, or the rescue of a person buried under rubble, then you are going to need strong men.

> *The strongest men are those who break the grasp of sin by receiving help from God and others.*

The strongest men are those who break the grasp of sin by receiving help from God and others.

I believe in men who look for help. I believe in men who still need tons of help. Men become real men, fully adult and mature when they get on their knees as Trent did and cry out for help from God. Trent went from being a 15-year-old setting a car on fire to being a man of God who sets people around the whole world on fire for Christ by the power of the Holy Spirit; or Jim Sumner who got on his knees in a jail cell confessing and repenting to God. Don't underestimate what God will do through you.

> *Don't underestimate what God will do through you.*

Application

1. What would it look like for you to rise above the times we live in? After reading Trent's story, what do you need to change?

   Action Item: Are you ready to stoke a fire and be a man on fire for Jesus Christ? Trent and his group hosted "burn parties" and I had a beach bonfire to get rid of all my old stuff. Do you have stuff that needs to be burned?

2. If you want full freedom, then take all your raunchy movies and music that bring back memories that need to be removed from your life and delete them from all your digital devices and cloud storage. Say goodbye to your memorabilia, whatever needs to go—whether it is a gift, an item, or even a valuable piece of jewelry—get rid of it all!

My Wife's Weekly Monday Fasting & Prayer

In the Fall of 2021, Jim and I learned about several close friends whose young adult children were not walking with God. It seemed like each week another name was added to my list of young adults to pray for, most of whom were women in their twenties. One evening as Jim shared his story with a group of parents, I met one mom who not only prayed for her daughter but fasted every Monday that she would be freed from her immoral sexual lifestyle.

I was so inspired by this mom's wisdom and humble release of her daughter into God's good care. I knew I was supposed to join her in fasting and lifting these young women up in prayer, all of whom I already knew by name. I remembered that twenty years ago my sister-in-law prayed and fasted for my Jim before I even met him when he was not walking with God. Jim Domen returned to the Lord and now his story of restoration gives hope.

Because my sister-in-law had so much love for her brother-in-law twenty years ago—God was awakening in me the same love for these young women.

I had confirmation in my heart that I was supposed to pray for each young adult by name and fast every Monday for their restoration. Over the past year, I have been learning how to fast and seeing how God uses it to change my heart. I cry out for mercy and hope for many other families who are waiting on God (Psalm 130:5). And I often meditate on Psalm 121, asking our Creator, whose design for creation cries out the truth, to protect these young lives.

- Amanda Domen

First time commitment to Jesus

If you're reading this book and do not know Jesus, I would love to take this opportunity to invite you to know him. If you decide to follow Jesus, he will change your life forever!

If you are saying "Yes" to Jesus, let me lead you in a prayer of confession, repentance, and transformation. Pray this out loud:

Jesus, thank you for dying on the cross and forgiving me of all my sins past, present and future.

I'd like to confess the sins of: [share your sins out loud to him].

I repent! What I mean by repenting is that I am choosing life and choosing to live differently according to your Scripture, the Bible.

I am making you Savior and Lord of my life today!

Jesus, help me walk in my new self as a new creation and my new identity in You. Help me find men to grow and disciple me so my roots grow deep.

In the all-powerful name of Jesus, AMEN!

Welcome to the family of Christ!

Date:_____

Signature: _____

Renewal commitment to Jesus:

If you are reading and feel the Holy Spirit tugging at your heart to refresh your relationship with Jesus, Laminations 3:22-23 says, "The steadfast love of the Lord never ceases; his mercies never come to an end; they are new every morning; great is your faithfulness." You can do so by saying this prayer out loud:

Jesus, I need you and realize my constant need for help. Thank you that your mercies are new every morning and you are faithful even when I am not. Please don't let my sin distract me from my true identity. Thank you that I have been forgiven since the beginning of time. Help me realize that I am not defined by my temptation and that my identity and freedom are only in you. In your name, Jesus. Amen.

Date:_____

Signature: _____

FINAL ENCOURAGEMENTS

It is imperative to break free of the sin habit — not just for ourselves, but for the generations after us. When you bring a little one into this world, as Amanda and I have, you can't help but start thinking beyond yourself. As a parent, it's no longer just about you. Suddenly, you realize you don't have the option to mess around and keep your favorite sin habits, because each sin we ignore will be one our children will also have to overcome, or at least forgive.

> ...because each sin we ignore will be one our children will also have to overcome, or at least forgive.

Generational sin is real. Deuteronomy 5:9-10 states: "I, the Lord your God, am a jealous God, punishing the children for the sin of the parents to the third and fourth generation of those who hate me, but showing love to a thousand generations of those who love me and keep my commandments."

Regardless of how one interprets the exact phrase "generational sin," the basic principle remains: Sins that aren't dealt with in one generation become that much harder for the next to overcome. I can't tell you how many times I've seen this play out with people I've coached and mentored. They'll talk about how their dad was an abusive alcoholic and now *they themselves* have the same struggle.

Thankfully, change is possible. My mom was a generational sin stopper. Her parents were divorced twice and each married three times. This pattern had been repeated for at least two generations back to my great-grandmother on my mom's side. Incredibly, my mom is the only one in her blended family of five whose marriage did not end in divorce. She has been married to my dad for over fifty years!

With God's help, Mom stopped the generational and spiritual stronghold of divorce that wreaked havoc and dysfunction in her family. You can do the same, but only with God's help.

Be a man who humbly seeks help. You may be surprised, but I have seen firsthand that when men respect their constant need for help, God incarnates them to be invincible.

Breaking Free of Shame: One Woman's Story

This is a book primarily directed to men, but I want to close with one woman's story to emphasize that women have their own spiritual strongholds with which to wrestle and bring under the Lordship of Christ. My mother's journey to becoming a "sin stopper" reminds me of a friend of mine, Nada Higuera. Nada (pronounced Netta) is a constitutional lawyer who represents churches and ministries in court. Today, she has a strong Christian husband and two beautiful kids, but her life did not always look this way.

Growing up in a Palestinian Islamic family, Nada was the youngest of eight girls. Because her parents desperately wanted a boy, she had this pervasive sense that she was unwanted. Her belief solidified when a friend of her family sexually abused her from the age of six until age fifteen. Only after Nada became pregnant did her parents confront her abuser. Her parents then forced her to have an abortion, which compounded her feelings of guilt.

When Nada turned 18, she heard the gospel for the first time, though it wasn't until her sophomore year in college that she started to attend church. Eventually, she received Christ and confessed that He is Lord; however, she still clung to her Muslim heritage and became engaged to a Muslim man. The two of them, however, realized that their faiths were incompatible and that is when her fiancé ended their engagement. Nada was devastated, but God began to heal her in unexpected ways that were far more wonderful than she had the capacity to imagine.

Years later, in 2015, the state of California passed the Reproductive FACT Act, which essentially forced pro-life pregnancy centers to direct their clients to abortion clinics. Then in 2017, Nada, now a lawyer, defended a Christian, pro-life, pregnancy center in Murrieta, California. But as she did, all those old feelings of guilt were engulfed in shame. Nada felt like a fraud because of her past abortion. Eventually, she came forward and publicly shared her story. To her surprise, she found incredible healing and peace by being open and truthful, that is, by walking in the light (I John 1:7).

Nada shared in a CBN article: "I was afraid of the shame, just having to feel that, when this all happened, and God redeemed that, I felt set free, redeemed. The word that kept coming to my mind is redeemed."[41]

Nada loves God. Through the power of Christ, she has broken the generational curse just as my mother did, though Nada's story obviously is different. Nada seeks to glorify God. Still, as she shares, she admits that sexual sin is a constant thorn in her side:

> I genuinely love God and seek to glorify Him. But sexual sin is a constant thorn in my side. My flesh desires sexual sin. It wages war against my spirit every day. Behind the lure of the seductiveness of my fleshly desires, I know sin is destructive to

---

41 https://www1.cbn.com/pro-life-advocate-healed-hidden-shame

myself, my husband, my kids, and mostly that it is an affront to God. But despite my knowledge, when my flesh is waging war against my spirit, sometimes it feels like giving in is the best option. However, when I give in by letting my mind go where it should not, the result is always the same. I gain temporary pleasure and emotional relief, but then I feel empty and distant from the God I love.

I have been a Christian for 15 years. I have fervently prayed for God to deliver me and remove the thorn. And while I can see his work of sanctification in me and His hand at work in my life, I thought my temptations would get easier. I thought my desire to sin would go away. Surely, I am not going to struggle for the rest of my life, right?

But despite prayer, fasting, deliverance, and counseling, the temptation has not gone away. But I am not defined by my temptation. Resistance is exhausting—when I try to resist in my own strength. If I isolate myself, I get discouraged that I still struggle. It feels lonely because I do not feel comfortable sharing with other women what my true battle is while the other women in my Bible study are praying for contentment and patience, I am silently praying that I won't follow the wicked desire of my flesh to commit sexual sin. It always feels like my sin and struggle is much, much worse than the godly Christian women around me.

The good news is that God has me in the palm of His righteous right hand. My sin and flesh have already been defeated. I know who the winner is: it's me, through Christ. I know that God is even using my sin to remind me of His grace and mercy. I also understand that I am not alone. How many other women are like me? We might feel alone, but that is deception. Sexual sin is not confined to men.

FINAL ENCOURAGEMENTS

Although Nada is still learning to trust in Christ completely to cleanse her of all sin, when God looks at Nada, he sees his pure, spotless, blameless daughter clothed in the righteousness of Christ.

It's the righteousness of Christ that we put on when we "put on our new self." We are not alone. Never, never alone because of Jesus. "Lo, I am with you always," Jesus said (Matthew 28:20b NASB 1995).

At the end of the day, the good news of the gospel produces a desire in the human spirit to love and obey God. Even when Nada stumbles and falls, the Lord picks her up. As Nada shares, "No power of hell, no scheme of man, can ever pluck me from His hand."

Every day Nada grows in the likeness of Christ. For her, the main challenge is to resist being alone. To ask for help from others. To risk being the only person in the Bible Study group who has her struggle.

I fully predict that when Nada's forthcoming book comes out that publicizes her struggle, droves of Christian women and men from other religions and no religion at all are going to be confessing that they can relate to her struggle.

According to Nada, "The biggest myth people have of God is that God's love for us is tied to our actions or the way we feel," she shares. "It's completely independent of those things."

"The biggest myth people have of God is that God's love for us is tied to our actions or the way we feel."

A Husband's Prayer for His Wife: Grant's Prayer for Nada

Lord, you are sovereign over our ongoing struggle with sin. Thank you that Nada knows her own weakness and continues to rely on your grace for her eternal salvation and your power in her daily life. The power that raised Jesus from the dead, lives in her. Help Nada know and be comforted by the truth that she could be no more loved by you than she already is. You know our past, present, and even future sins. And yet, you still sent your Son to suffer and die in our place. Give Nada comfort and rest in knowing that you, the author and perfecter of her faith, rejoice over her, for you only see the beauty of Your Son's righteousness in her. Preserve her and bless our marriage. Draw us evermore closer to you and to one another.

- Grant Higuera

Be a Generational Sin Blocker

Like Nada and my mom, you too can be a generational sin blocker. You can know what it means to have your sins forgiven. You don't have to live in shame; you can break the habit of sin in your life and leave a legacy of faithfulness to your children.

In this book, I've done my best to offer seven practical steps you can take to break the habit of sin in your life. Believe me when I say these steps work! No, they aren't easy. Yes, they require attention and focus, but if you follow this pattern I have outlined, I am confident you can experience the same freedom that I—and many others I've coached—have experienced.

FINAL ENCOURAGEMENTS

Application

Action Items

1. What steps do you need to take to embark on the path to freedom? Is there a CAMP-D (Coach, Accountability partner, Mentor, Pastor or Discipler) you can connect with?
2. Find *Desert Stream Ministries* in your area at *DesertStream.org* if you're dealing with any type of sexual issue.
3. Sign up for an online live 7-session coaching platform or in-person retreat at *JimDomen.com*.
4. Do not ride alone: Ride with others. Find a ministry with people who will journey with you.

Review the items below that were discussed previously in "Do Your Part:"

1. **Change** the stuff you listen to and watch. Which tunes or movies remind you of the life you used to live? Distance yourself from this material.
2. **Remove** social media apps on your phone that distract you.
3. **Get rid** of all material possessions connected to the sinful lifestyle you were living. If you've had sex multiple times in your bed, get rid of your old bed.
4. **Move!** Move to a new location so you don't pass those same places that brought you down or move away from people in your past.
5. **Delete** photos that no longer represent the life you have in Christ.

In the first chapter, you identified your issues. In this chapter, you read about the three paths:

1) Uncontrollable Addiction,
2) Unhealthy Behavior, and
3) Ultimate Freedom.

1. With which one of the three paths does your issue resonate? Your answer will help guide you in dealing with the severity of your sin's grasp.

2. What does ultimate freedom look like? Remember, your temptation does not define you!

Let's Recap

Step 1: Realize Why You Aren't Free
There was a moment when you first experienced your sinful behavior, and it still holds you captive. Certain triggers: Hungry, Angry, Lonely, Tired, Stressed, or Depressed (HALTS-D) can activate your sinful behavior. No matter where your story began, freedom is found in Christ alone. You must choose a right relationship with God and "walk in the Spirit" which is the powerful alternative to sinful living to have true freedom.

Step 2: Reach Out to a Church
Being part of a local church enables you to experience the blessings of different members in the body of Christ. A strong church body will help you remain focused on what is most important, even when you're tempted to give up. Finding the right church can be difficult. But as someone who visits a lot of churches for speaking engagements, I've found that great churches have several key characteristics. Great churches are Spirit-led congregations where regular life transformation takes place in its members. They are uncompromising in their view of God's Word. They are passionate about helping Christians become stronger disciples of Christ. Find a church that does these three things well, and it's likely you've found your home.

Step 3: Ride with Other Men
There are no lone rangers in God's kingdom. Even the Lone Ranger had Tonto! This means it's imperative to reach out to other guys and lean on them for strength. Riding by yourself makes you easy prey for the enemy. But riding with others makes you strong.

Step 4: Reorganize Your Schedule

Most people make poor decisions because they have poor systems in place to protect them against themselves. But if you really want to break your sinful habit, you've got to get radical. This might mean avoiding different places you used to like, activities you enjoyed, or devices that make it easy to fall into sin.

Step 5: Replace Bad Habits

It's time to put off the old self and put on the new. Make the decision to live differently for 90 days. Doing so won't be easy. There will be days you'll be tempted to give up. But stick with it. It is imperative to understand your true identity in Christ. Don't be distracted by your temptation and don't believe that is who you are. Break your destructive sin habit and establish a new one in its place.

Step 6: Retrain Your Brain

Along with replacing bad habits, it's vital that you learn to think differently. Everyone has different lies they believe which keep them from achieving their potential in Christ. Take the action steps to retrain your brain:

1. identify your major issue.
2. find a replacement.
3. plan for temptation and think strategically.
4. confess and repent if you stumble.

The key is to lean into our spiritual identity and ask the Holy Spirit to transform us by the renewing of our minds.

Step 7: Rise Above

Don't stop! Remember that you've never done too much or gone too far to outrun the grace of God. Confess, receive God's forgiveness, and believe in God's divine power to transform you. He still loves you and he *will* give you the strength you need to overcome any habit of sin you face. It's up to you to believe and trust him. Get rid of things from your past. Burn them!

I challenge you to start at the beginning and commit to the full measure in each of these steps. Make sure you don't take half-measures in any of these steps. Don't cheat yourself and think you can skip one and move on to the next. They all build on one another and to miss one will make it that much easier to miss others.

Start a Coaching Program

Because I believe in the power of riding with others, I invite you to an online coaching experience where a coach or I will walk you through the action steps mentioned in this book. Through our time together, we will confront the poor habits and develop a game plan for you to live in victory. For seven sessions we will meet every other week at a time and day of the week that fits your schedule. Learn more and sign up at **JimDomen.com.**

Another option is the Breaking Sin's Grasp men's retreat. This is a time when you can meet other men who are working with God to break free of their sinful habits. During our time together, a coach or I will take you and other attendees through seven sessions. A retreat would accomplish everything like the online courses but in an expedited manner. The retreats would require travel where you'd experience breaking free from sin's grasp face-to-face with other men.

Private, one-on-one coaching is available online or in person at your location of choice. Contact Jim for this option at JimDomen.com.

FINAL ENCOURAGEMENTS

The coaching topics include:

1. Share your story.
2. Timeline Experience.
3. Steps to Freedom in Christ.
4. Dump it!
5. Spiritual Gifts.
6. Strongholds (Restorative Prayer & Fasting).
7. Action Plan.

Whether you attend a retreat, do group online coaching, one-on-one private coaching or find your own coach, I would love to connect with you and hear more about your personal journey of breaking sin's grasp!

Do you want to be healed?

In His grace, truth, and freedom!

Jim

PS - Connect with me at JimDomen.com or scan this QR code.

AUTHOR'S NOTE

The stories contained in the book are of men I've journeyed with for over 20 years as a pastor. To protect their identities their names have been changed except for a few of the stories. If your name matches a story used, it's a coincidence. The stripper story of Jim Sumner; the drug dealer, porn addict, drug and alcoholic story of Pastor Trent Douglass and his brother; and sex abuse survivor Nada Higuera are their personal testimonies and their real names and are used with permission.

Prayers and comments from women are their real names. Nada Higuera's husband Grant is his real name.

Dr. Mark Legome passed away in 2022 and his wife Dr. Marty Myers wrote the note. Those are their true names.

If your temptation or sin issue(s) is not mentioned in this book, please do not be discouraged. I cannot include a story for every type of sin. Be assured, the road map to freedom is the same. It's provided in *Breaking Sin's Grasp, Your Temptation Doesn't Define You*, and the pathway to freedom is Jesus and can be applied to any sin(s).

Hear my story, get a study guide, watch a video series, read other books, or request me to speak at your church or event at JimDomen.com.

ABOUT THE AUTHOR

Jim Domen has pastored for over 20 years, receiving his Master of Divinity from Azusa Pacific University in 2008. He is an Ironman completing an Ironman distance triathlon: swimming 2.4 miles, cycling 112 miles and running 26.2 miles; body builder, a Recorded Conservative Evangelical Friends Pastor, and founder of ChurchUnited.com that disrupts pastors to speak truth to power. Jim is a contributing author to the Epoch Times and The Christian Post. He and Amanda, his wife of over fifteen years, have three children.

Sign-up for coaching at JimDomen.com